WORKING
WOMAN'S
Art of War

WORKING WOMAN'S Art of War

winning without confrontation

Chin-Ning Chu

Author of the international best-selling books:
Do Less Achieve More, Thick Face Black Heart,
The Asian Mind Game

For information address: **AMC Publishing,**
PO Box 2986, Antioch, CA 94531 USA
Telephone: (925) 777-1888; Fax: (925) 777-1238
e-mail: cnc@strategic.org | website: www.strategic.org

Library of Congress Cataloging–in–Publication Data

Chin-Ning Chu
  Working Woman's Art of War: winning without
confrontation / Chin-Ning Chu.
    ISBN 0-929638-29-8
    1. New Feminism—Women's studies. I. Title.
    2. Women's work strategy—Business, etc.
    3. Women's success—Business, Women's studies, etc.
    4. Art of war—Business, Philosophy, etc.
    3. Women's Leadership—Business, Women's studies, etc.

Cover design by Darren Savage of Savage Graphics
Author photo by Edward Chang

Printed in the United States of America
10 9 8 7 6 5 4 3 2 1

People are saying...

"Chin-Ning, write more books."
—Gurumayi, SYDA Foundation

"Chin-Ning has been a follower of spiritual teachings that are closely aligned with Mahatma Gandhi's for decades. In *Working Woman's Art of War*, she has unleashed women's innate power to achieve their noble objectives of equality and moral supremacy. Yet, while her strategy is internally challenging to the practitioners, it remains always externally peaceful towards others."
—Kristi Gandhi, Co-Founder,
Women WorldWide

"Once again, Chin-Ning Chu provides a strategic road-map to making important choices and the tools of Tao to back your decisions."
—Marquetta Glass, Diversity Relations &
Strategy Director, Hallmark Cards

"*Working Woman's Art of War* is what women need for this century. Thank you for this wonderful insight and guidance. I can now comfortably get away with wearing one glass slipper and one combat boot—to a Ball or the Boardroom."
—Erin L. Mac Arthur, Director,
Pacific Asia Travel Association

"*Working Woman's Art of War* continues Chin-Ning's tradition of excellence established by her prior best-selling books. She combines depth of knowledge and insights to encourage women to turn liabilities into assets and achieve their full potential, both professionally and at home."
—Caroline Marks, Commissioner,
San Francisco Commission on the Status of Women

"*Working Woman's Art of War* is a guidebook that dispenses a powerful perspective and dynamic strategies for each woman to get ahead, and to be ecstatically happier in the Twenty-first Century."
—Sonal Patwari,
Mahatma Gandhi's Great Grandniece

OTHER BOOKS BY CHIN-NING CHU

The Asian Mind Game
Thick Face, Black Heart
Do Less, Achieve More

I want to express my heartfelt appreciation to the following people for their assistance in completing this book:

Greg & Susan Bolt,

Caroline Pinkus,

Joan Egloff-Olson

Naresh K. Bali,

Lee Doolan,

Sir Yogesh Gandhi,

Matthew & Robin Goldworm,

Susan Kline,

Caroline Marks,

Ashish Parekh,

Parth Patwari,

and Theresa Sawyer.

CONTENTS

*This book is not about five steps to this or that;
it embodies paradoxes, choices.*

*Like walking on the beach,
exploring the different colors
and shapes of the sea shells,
picking the ones that
appeal to you most—experimenting,
trying them out,
finding the ones that work for you.*

*You may see that different ideas and strategies
will appeal to you upon different readings.*

*This book, then,
will serve you for a lifetime.*

HAVING IT ALL WITH THE ART OF WAR

Before waging a war,
the five essential elements
that govern success must be examined.
Only then can a proper assessment be done.

Number One—Tao (Righteousness),
Two—Tien (Timing),
Three—Di (Earth),
Four—Jiang (Leadership),
Five—Fa (Managing).
—Sun Tzu (1.2)

1

Regardless of what men think about how much they know of women, only a woman knows how difficult it is to be a woman. Besides having a complex emotional and physical composition, as working women, we are also income providers that play the multiple role of wife, mother, cook, janitor, crises manager, bookkeeper, accountant, teacher, laundry service, gardener, chauffeur, healer, psychiatrist, physician, dish washer, and trash collector for our families.

In the last century everyone told us it was impossible for a woman to have everything she wanted; that the process of pursuing "having it all" was causing us to become physically overwhelmed and left suffering from mental indigestion. We women, in order to compete in this male-dominated world, have always had to be twice as good at our jobs as comparable men while taking one-third less pay.

The times they are a'changing. After the battle of the genders waged during the last century, every woman is more secure than ever in her feminine self. Unlike our mothers, most women today have a big appetite for life—and the will to express these appetites.

Recently, I was in Sydney, Australia, where a billboard for a career placement agency caught my attention. It read: "Before, I just wanted to marry a millionaire. Now, I want to become one." This attitude is not only expressed in Australia and United States, this has become an international phenomenon—a bond of universal womanhood that cuts across and beyond cultures and national boundaries.

This book is not against men. We love men. I am especially indebted to many men who, throughout my career, have given me the lift that I needed for no other motive than they genuinely appreciated my work. Herein, we will examine strategies which support every woman in celebrating our feminine selves to the fullest while we gain the total freedom to soar to our personal and professional heights.

It is well known that our male counterparts embrace the concepts of war and battle like fish take to water. For thousands of years men have fought life's battles. Genetically their minds have been imprinted to think like warriors.

In the West, we think of war as turning loose opposing troops to bash each other. At the end of the battle, we count the bodies. The winning side is the one with the greatest number of soldiers still standing. When we hear "the art of war," we think of battle, casualties, brutality.

However, the Chinese concept of the art of war, which dates back three thousand five hundred years, is not about war; it is a set of strategies for attaining peace and victory that emphasize doing everything in the easiest possible way. It is a set of mental maneuvering skills for achieving your desired outcome with the least possible output of effort.

These art of war strategies are a perfect match for women's greatest natural strengths. For thousands of years, women living in male-dominated societies have learned the value of appearing submissive in order to conquer. We allow men to think they are in charge, when in fact we often get our way by pretending to go along with them. Intuitively, women have always used some of the Chinese art of war strategies in maneuvering and negotiating with our husbands, lovers, children, bosses, friends, customers and clients. We just didn't know we were actually strategists in disguise. It is about time that we learn the full spectrum of the art of war.

Among all the ancient strategy treaties, and there were many, Sun Tzu's *Art of War*, written around 460 B.C., is the most popular in business today. I chose this text, once used to determine the fates of nations, to guide women in adapting some of its potent strategies to help us win the battles of gender inequality, personal acceptance, work place prejudice, balancing of family and job duties, and managing our children and office. I didn't choose Sun Tzu's *Art of War* solely because of its popularity; I chose it for its power, for its phenomenal record of success.

History has proven the art of war a success. Sun Tzu was not a military man when he wrote his art of war treaties. He was a farmer by profession and a self-taught philosopher. He wrote the *Sun Tzu Bing Fa* (*Bing* means soldier, *fa* means skill) as a résumé in the hopes of getting a job as the King of Wu's military commander. After the King of Wu employed him as the military commander, Sun Tzu put his strategy text to the test.

During one battle, with an army of only 30,000 men, Sun Tzu defeated the Kingdom of Zhou, who had a contingent of 300,000 men. In 482 B.C., twenty years after he first became employed by the King of Wu, Sun Tzu proved the superiority of his strategies when he conquered the twelve Chinese nations, enabling his militarily inferior employer to become the supreme ruling power of China. (Twenty years may sound like a long time to the American ear, but consider that Sun Tzu was working in the midst of a Chinese civil war that would last nearly six hundred years, so twenty years was nothing!)

After Sun Tzu died, King Wu's successor lost control of China, and not until 221 B.C., two hundred sixty one years later, did China once again come under one dominating ruler, Emperor Chin, the emperor made famous as the builder of the Great Wall and for his terra cotta tomb. Putting this in historical perspective, you can see that controlling China was no small task.

In 1772 Sun Tzu's *Art of War* was translated into French. It is widely believed that Napoleon read and adopted many of Sun Tzu's strategies. During Desert Storm (the conflict between Iraq and the United States in 1990-1991), every officer in the U.S. Marines was issued a copy of the *Art of War* as standard battle gear.

The art of war is universal; it is about the art, not the war. For five thousand years, Chinese philosophers had devoted their time to observing and documenting nature's secrets and the subtle patterns that govern it. Sun Tzu based his *Art of War* principles on these philosophical observations of the laws governing the universe.

Like the philosophers before him, Sun Tzu saw that these principles applied to any situation. It has never been more true than in today's business world, where every transaction is like bloodless warfare. More important still, Sun Tzu's *Art of War* is not only about competition, but applies equally well to managing office politics and motivating your children.

Sun Tzu's *Art of War* may be ancient, but it is eternal. In fact, I am always surprised that no one until now has written a book about how women can adopt Sun Tzu's *Art of War* to our every situation. As Sun Tzu put it: *"The best among the best of strategies is winning without fighting."* Now what in *that* wouldn't appeal to every woman?

5

Sun Tzu's *Art of War* is just thirteen chapters long, its first chapter serving as a kind of summary of the whole book. In the first chapter, Sun Tzu speaks of the importance of five essential art of war elements:

One should adopt the five elements as the foundation of warfare. By examining the following five elements I can know the outcome of a war:
> 1. *Tao (moral standing, righteousness)*
> 2. *Tien (climatic conditions, timing)*
> 3. *Di (earth, assets and liabilities)*
> 4. *Jian (leadership)*
> 5. *Fa (managing and discipline)*

I have organized this book around these five foundational elements. As you enter each element, you will discover the kinds of issues in our everyday lives as women, mothers, and working women for which the *Art of War* so brilliantly applies.

By being proficient in the art of war strategies, you will see what your competitor does not see, and hear the silent messages that your competitor cannot hear. Your mind will travel along strategic byways that your competitors will find impenetrable.

You can become a proficient female strategist whether you set your sights on being a corporate CEO, entrepreneur, school teacher, stock broker, movie producer, or astronaut. If your aim in life is to be a happy woman and good mother (and this is a noble aim indeed), the study of the art of war can provide you with the strategies to turn your life's disadvantages into advantages, and even assist you in cultivating well-disciplined, well-focused children.

In order for women to have all that we want—the right to choose to wear glass slippers and/or combat boots—we need to have the courage to learn how to think like effective strategists and warriors.

This book is full of strategies and ideas for women to get ahead, and making choices. With these ancient tools, every woman, whether she works at home or in the office, can become a wildly innovative, rapidly adaptive, brilliantly creative, happy, fun-loving winner.

Chin-Ning Chu

I. TAO—RIGHTEOUSNESS

Armed with the sense of righteousness
and the blessings from Heaven,
your army becomes fearless.
Thus, they are willing to live and
die for the purpose of realizing victory.
                    —Sun Tzu (1.3)

*Many persons have a wrong idea of
what constitutes true happiness.
It is not attained through self-gratification,
but through fidelity to a worthy purpose.*
—Helen Keller

THE TAO OF STRATEGY

Those who carefully calculate their strategies,
will be led to victory.
Those who carelessly calculate their strategies,
will be led to defeat.
—Sun Tzu (1.28)

It is not by accident that Sun Tzu placed *tao* as the first element of strategy. Of the art of war strategies, *tao* is the most important element for victory. *Tao* means "the way, rightness or morality" and it is also much more than that. *Tao* is defined as the force behind all creation. As the foremost Taoist philosopher, Lao Tzu said, *"I do not know what to call Her, I call Her 'tao.'"* All things good, brilliant, righteous, creative, innovative, ecstatic, sweet and joyful are rooted in *tao*.

Without *tao*, no matter how clever you are, all you have going for you will be merely a bag of dirty tricks. Without *tao*, the more you maneuver, the more you can get yourself into trouble. You should not even think of using strategies without first adopting *tao* into your daily life.

The leaders of every major war and minor battle have always claimed that they were the righteous ones because no one will follow you if you can't convince everyone that you represent the will of Heaven. Even a satanic tyrant such as Hitler had to persuade the German people that he was leading them to glory. However, patriotic slogans can only take you so far, eventually, the truth will prevail.

Throughout human history, whoever has betrayed *tao*, has always ultimately been defeated. On September 21, 1999, for example, a 7.4 earthquake shook Taiwan and exposed the shoddy practices of unethical builders who for years had been cutting corners and reaping enormous profits. It turns out that they had been filling structural beams with nothing more than empty plastic soy sauce bottles and aluminum cooking-oil cans. Many of these builders will be criminally prosecuted for intentionally harming the public. In just 30 seconds, *tao* caught up with them.

Tao is the foundation of the other four elements—*tien, di, jiang* and *fa*. Without *tao*, you can't even begin to discuss the other four. If you cannot convince yourself and your people that your cause is right and moral—give up the project; you can't win. In later chapters we will explore more about how *tao* directly effects your personal success as a working woman, entrepreneur, corporate executive, saleswoman or stay-at-home mother. In the meantime, we will focus on the *tao* of strategy.

Strategy is really about common sense. In every project and situation, there is a rightness, an integrity, and that rightness is *tao*. If you can find out how to reach that rightness, you have adopted the *tao* of strategies. Do the right thing and the right result will come—in its own time.

The Basic Principles Of Strategy:

1. The Roots of Strategic Thinking Can Be Found in Nature

Give your opponent the impression,
you are as shy as a virgin,
so they will underestimate you.
This will cause them to lack vigilance,
and provide you with an opening.
Pattern yourself after the escaping rabbit,
so your opponent will be caught by surprise.
Thus, they will not be able to defend themselves.
—Sun Tzu (11.70)

For five thousand years, the Chinese philosophers and art of war masters have been observing and documenting how the secrets of nature unfold. One cannot discern the subtleties of nature's patterns over a single lifetime or in the span of a few hundred years. Ultimately, these philosophers and strategists discovered that the rhythm of nature is applicable to every aspect of one's life: it is unfailing and consistent, at ease within itself.

They discovered that the same principles that govern nature can be applied to the conducting of warfare, our business transactions and our home lives. Just as the laws of gravity, the changing of the seasons, the earth revolving around the sun are consistent and dependable, so is strategy when applied appropriately.

The great strategists have learned to identify and attune themselves to the principles at work in nature and see how nature's principles can be transported to everything we do in life. For example, water is soft and yields to rock, but over time water will erode rock; a blade of grass will sway with a strong wind and not break, yet a mighty 500 years old oak tree is firm and unyielding and can be uprooted by the same wind. There is great strength in the ability to yield. A person or a country can become unconquerable through yielding.

The Japanese adopted nature's principle of yielding after WWII in order to successfully dominate the American home electronics industry. By Japan acting humble, using the strategy of "pretending to be a pig in order to eat the tiger", America was led to underestimate Japan's ambition and her threat to the U.S. economic sector.

Tao recognizes the single, unifying principle in the diverse manifestations that exist throughout the universe. Einstein's and subsequent physicists' search for a Unified Field Theory is based on the same line of thinking. As Einstein once said, "All I want to know is how God created the universe. All the rest are minor details."

2. The Small Can Overcome the Mighty

When a victory is won
through the obvious advantage
of outnumbering of the enemy,
the victor deserves no praise.
Under these circumstances,
when a warrior succeeds in battle,
that warrior deserves no praise.
Lifting thin air is not an indication
of one's strength.
Seeing the sun and the moon
does not indicate sharp vision.
Hearing thunder does not indicate
superior hearing.

—Sun Tzu (4.8)

Imagine a huge rock resting on the edge of a cliff. Sitting there, it has no power, but with just the tiniest effort to push it off the cliff you can liberate the tremendous force of the rock. The reason a sitting rock and a falling rock exhibit two totally different powers has to do with the momentum caused by gravity and the precision used in how you push the rock.

Any small and inferior force that can incorporate momentum and precision of delivery will have the power to overcome the mighty and the powerful. David defeated the giant Goliath with the momentum of David's sling and the precision of his release.

The recent miraculous success of the lingerie company Victoria's Secret is a perfect example of using momentum to create success. Women have always worn undergarments yet, prior to Victoria's Secret, no one had made a great hit by selling women's underwear.

Women's undergarments were like a rock sitting on the edge of a cliff. The momentum came from women's new-found fashion obsession, along with our modern figure consciousness and our willingness to spend the money to look our best. Victoria's Secret's design and catalogue marketing concept was the tiny bit of effort needed to push the rock off the cliff.

The objective of the use of a strategy is to enhance the success rate of the inferior. Prior to Victoria's Secret, underwear truly qualified as something "not so important." Yet, with the precision send off and the momentum of the consumer's unvoiced desires, the "insignificant" underwear company conquered the mighty fashion industry.

By learning from the example of the falling rock, we can see that by using just the tiniest effort, we can liberate our own momentum toward accomplishing our noblest of aims.

3. Strategy Is Defensive as Well as Offensive

When the victory is not certain,
adopt defensive tactics;
when the odds for victory are overwhelming,
adopt offensive tactics.
—Sun Tzu (4.5)

Whenever I visit my friend May in Hong Kong, she is always jokingly telling me that she is going to make some money that afternoon. The way May makes money is to play *mahjong* with some friends for amusement. In order to make the game interesting, they play for up to a hundred dollars per game. No doubt, she always ends up a winner. I asked her how she so consistently does it and she told me, "When I feel lucky, I take chances by playing an aggressive game of offence. When my luck is not with me, I play a defensive game." Sun Tzu's principles work in warfare as well as at the mahjong table and in the business world.

In business, proficiency in the art of strategy is not only about imposing your will on others; it is also about having at your command a vital defensive tool. In order to prevent yourself from falling prey to another's deceptive plots, you must first, as a defensive tool, learn how to recognize and detect their tricky strategies.

If being aggressive is not your style, strategy can still serve you as a defensive tool to protect you from other people's dirty tricks. When the people in your life always play dumb or humble for no apparent reason—very loyal, very sweet, very subservient—it is easy to be conned. By understanding strategies, you will think twice about their motives and watch them throughout your engagement.

4. One Who Is Going to Use Strategy Needs Impeccable Morality

Unless you are aligned with tao,
and have impeccable morality,
you will not know how to use spies.
                              —*Sun Tzu (13.14)*

In order to recognize the crooked intentions of your opponent, you need to be very strict yourself, with an unshakable ethic and a strong set of moral values. Only against the backdrop of your clear, undiffused integrity can you see how crooked others are.

A person with a crooked perspective sees crooked people as straight; she cannot identify who is good and who is bad, who is moral and who is immoral. Strategies are just a bag of dirty tricks unless you possess *tao*. Without *tao*, the more you try to use strategy, the more it will backfire on you.

This is why Sun Tzu believes, for one to utilize spies in gathering information for you, you need to have impeccable moral standards. If you are immoral, you will not recognize if the spy you are using has his/her loyalty with you or with your enemy. Thus, the information you get could be faulty or harmful to your campaign.

Studying the *tao* of strategy will help you to bring forth your brilliant ideas on the job and in your home. The *tao* which is the force that directs the military general in winning the battle also directs the proficient business woman or politician in exercising her power. It also will make you more aware of the workings of nature, which will become your constant teacher.

You will learn how to challenge yourself to recognize and translate nature's movements into flexible, ingenious strategies. While it is good to learn strategies; it is even better to have the innate ability to invent strategies at will. By learning to do so, you will be motivated to become wildly innovative in all of your life's varied endeavors and have much more fun in your professional, personal and family life.

Adopt these strategies within with great care and with great integrity. Then, the strategies will serve you and support your every step.

You can do one of two things:
just shut up,
which is something I don't find easy,
or learn an awful lot very fast
which is what I tried to do.
                    —Jane Fonda

WHO SAYS IT'S O.K. TO PUT WOMEN DOWN?

Within the universe,
there are no eternal conquerors.
The sun provides short and long days,
and the moon has waxing and waning cycles.
—Sun Tzu (6.26)

In the universe, *yin* (the female force) is equal to *yang* (the male force). As Lao Tzu, the great Taoist philosopher said, "*The universe, carrying yin and yang in her bosom, infuses both forces with equal energy. Thus, harmony is created.*" Heaven did not create the inequality between the genders, but the major blame, at least for the ills of the past, must be attributed to men. I want to make sure that everyone knows I am not speaking against men, and that this book is not about men-bashing. However, since human history is about his-story, and it was written and interpreted by men, that is where the problem began.

Anything against *tao* will ultimately seek its own destruction. This is a universal law. Keeping anybody down—by differences of culture, religion, gender, skin color—is against *tao*. Therefore keeping women down is not *tao*. It will seek its own destruction or correction. Guaranteed.

In early times, to ensure that the human species survived, men were built for physical strength and the power to hunt while women were specialized for the propagation and nurturing of babies. Considering the elements needed for survival in that prehistoric period, this was the most appropriate method for the division of duties. However, this in itself did not create a male-dominated society because females could still have been the hierarchical rulers. Ruling, administering, and managing do not require physical power.

Xian, the cradle of Chinese civilization, is commonly known to Westerners as the city where the giant terra-cotta statues were found and was President Clinton's first stop during his visit to China in

1998. I have had the opportunity to view this fascinating excavation site outside of Xian. Sixty-five hundred years ago, an ancient, highly civilized society existed there. It is the site of the oldest complete society ever discovered in China—and this advanced civilization was a matriarchal society.

In this city, females conducted the town meetings and carried out all of the administrative duties while the males did the work which required physical strength such as hunting and constructing housing—the manual labor. Could it be that nature intended for men to hunt, but that the higher responsibility of managing the clan should be given to women? In ancient Chinese, Etruscans, and Cretin civilizations, among others, woman's position was certainly more than equal. Let's look at what other false biases contribute to the present-day prejudices against women.

Men rely on the following to keep women down:

• Valuing Competitiveness over Empathy and Cooperation

Competition gives instant gratification and creates tangible results. Empathy and cooperation, on the other hand, may make us feel an inner harmony but produce no outward gratification. Going all the way back to the days of the cave dwellers, men have competed, women have empathized.

When two females get together they try to make one another feel comfortable. A tall woman standing next to a short woman will unconsciously stoop to become a little shorter so that the shorter one might feel more at ease. The majority of females prefer to co-exist in harmony with their surroundings rather than be egotistically dominating and acting viciously confrontational.

During a power lunch I attended, a waiter dropped a stack of dishes that broke into pieces on the tile floor. I noticed the pain on his face and my heart leaped out to him. At the same time, I also observed my three male counterparts sitting with me at the same table didn't miss a beat; they carried on as if nothing had happened.

A friend of mine told me a similar story. While she was a guest of honor during a conference, a flag on the stage fell. Although she didn't move, she noticed her first reaction was to pick up the flag while the male guests on the stage displayed their normal stoic attitudes.

From the beginning of time, in order to insure her infant's survival, a mother needed to quickly develop the skill of understanding the silent communication of her baby and to be empathetic to her infant's feelings. This caused her to become more considerate; reaching out towards others' suffering.

Contrary to females, males are more self-centered and competitive. When two men get together, they compete with each other so as to quickly establish the pecking order. The tall one stands taller; the strong one quickly displays his might by flashing his muscles; the quick-witted engage in verbal assaults. They are more animalistic and, like the male apes, compete for the dominant position. Living through the armpit of human evolution, the subtle feminine qualities have been held hostage by crude, brutal male assertions.

Our society glorifies the ego and competition over empathy and cooperation. The principle of *tao* is the opposite. All fine things are subtle, intangible. It's important for women not to buy into the glorification of ego. Empathy and cooperation will be the superior qualities in the 21st century. Don't lose sight of that in your quest for power.

• The Venom of the Holy Doctrines

It is absurd to contemplate that women are spiritually inferior in any way, but some of the men who first organized religious doctrine seem to have decided that women are an inferior species and have interpreted our holy books from that point of view.

Does anyone really believe that Mary Magdalene is relegated to a second level of heaven while the rest of Christ's disciples live on the first? The fact that Mary Magdalene did not travel with Christ at all times only means that she was bound by the cultural and social practices of her time and could not sleep on open ground. But this fact did not mean she was spiritually inferior—that is only how events were later interpreted.

Some religious leaders say she was not invited to the Last Supper (as this event was depicted in Leonardo Da Vinci's famous interpretation). Could this be because she was so spiritually advanced that she did not need the formality of bread and wine to be connected to her devotion to Christ? An advanced spiritual being is never separate from her beloved divine master; she is constantly aligned with God.

There also exist certain discrepancies and differing interpretations of what exactly happened on that fateful night over two millennia ago. For the PBS show, "From Jesus to Christ," Professor L. Michael White—the Religious Studies Program Director for the University of Texas at Austin—tells of the mosaic in the Church of Santa Podenziana at Rome, "Here, we have what looks at first to be a very traditional scene from the gospels; Jesus is seated in the middle of his apostles flanked along either side of him. It looks very much like a kind of Last Supper scene, and yet you notice that there are two women seated behind, ... It's probably the Virgin Mary and Mary Magdalene..."

Also consider that on the day when Christ resurrected from the dead, he appeared to Mary Magdalene first and alone. This is such a significant event, yet all of the Christian churches downplay it. By Christ appearing to Mary Magdalene not only acknowledges her devotion and courage (remember, she tended His body while all the male disciples went into hiding in fear of the Romans), it also acknowledges womankind at large.

His appearing to a woman symbolizes that he knew, out of woman's intuition and sensitivity, she would accept him without question—unlike his male disciples who later, upon meeting Christ, asked Him for proof that He was their Lord. It was no accident Christ chose to appear to Mary Magdalene as his first act after resurrection in his total Godhood. This was His way of acknowledging and honoring the uniqueness of womankind.

In the Nag Hammadi Library version of the Gnostic gospel, "The Gospel of Mary," Mary Magdalene is actually exalted above the rest of the disciples because Jesus had chosen to appear only before her in a vision.

"Peter said to Mary, 'Sister, we know that the Savior loved you more than the rest of women. Tell us the words of the Savior which you remember - which you know (but) we do not, nor have we heard them.'

"...When Mary had said this [told of her vision], she fell silent, since it was to this point that the Savior had spoken with her. But Andrew answered and said to the brethren, 'Say what you (wish to) say about what she has said. I at least do not believe that the Savior said this. For certainly these teachings are strange ideas.' Peter answered and spoke concerning these same things. He questioned them about the Savior: 'Did He really speak with a woman without our knowledge (and) not openly? Are we to turn about and all listen to her? Did He prefer her to us?'

"Then Mary wept and said to Peter, 'My brother Peter, what do you think? Do you think that I thought this up myself in my heart, or that I am lying about the Savior?' Levi answered and said to Peter, 'Peter, you have always been hot-tempered. Now I see you contending against the woman like the adversaries. But if the Savior made her worthy, who are you indeed to reject her?

" 'Surely the Savior knows her very well. That is why He loved her more than us. Rather let us be ashamed and put on the perfect man and acquire him for ourselves as He commanded us, and preach the gospel, not laying down any other rule or other law beyond what the Savior said.' ...and they began to go forth [to] proclaim and to preach."

Like Christianity, some sects of Buddhism also got it all wrong. The Chinese brand of Buddhism was imported from India, and then exported to Japan. Since, in ancient China, religion is heavily associated with male domination, naturally Buddhism became a male-dominated religion. Like Christianity, the priests and monks are at the top of the hierarchy while the nuns are the servants to their holier male counterparts.

The root of Buddhism is in Hinduism, and yet the Hindu religion sees God as female as well as male. The active energy that runs the world is symbolized by the feminine power of Shakti; the masculine aspect of God is symbolized by the dormant power of Shiva. That male energy Shiva without the female energy Shakti would remain immobile.

27

Even with their holy doctrine as such, many Hindu temples still prohibit women from entering and worshiping when the women are on their menstrual periods. I wonder if the temple priests have ever asked the Goddess, their object of worship, when her period is due so they might throw her statue out for a week until she becomes "clean."

• The Misinterpretation of Confucius

Every culture has its own tales of why women deserve to be held down. In Asia, where thirty percent of the world's population lives, people are heavily influenced by Confucius' teachings and conduct their own affairs according to their misinterpretations of his words.

The source of all the misunderstanding lies in this one sentence: "Women and ignorant men are hard to tangle with." Because of this statement, Asian women have been victimized for thousands of years, especially by Japanese and Korean men who are greater sticklers for the Confucian rules when it comes to practicing Chinese wisdom.

What puzzled me all my life was why Confucius, the greatest sage in all of Chinese history, would make a statement that was so purely sexist. I pondered this and finally the answer came. It was not that Confucius was sexist; it has always been, even unto the present, that those male scholars who interpret his words are sexist. I am absolutely certain that if Confucius were living today, he would not see women as inferiors.

Confucius lived approximately two thousand years ago. The ignorant men he referred to were hard to deal with because, although they studied, they did not embody the wisdom they had learned. The women were ignorant because they were not *allowed* to study. They were not allowed to think for themselves; society dictated how they should think and how they should act. A lot of ridiculous rules were imposed on them and the women accepted them without question.

Confucius' statement does not refer to women's inherent nature but to the ignorant plight of women in his time. After all, Confucius dedicated his life to righting the wrongs of society and those wrongs were there to be found all around him.

Like all great teachings, Confucius' teachings were rejected in his time by princes and commoners alike. Because of this, Confucius spoke harshly of the ignorance of both genders. Yet, somehow male interpreters down through the ages conveniently ignored the possibility of men being ignorant and focused only on the female species as inferior. This shows how ignorant men can be. If Confucius could rise today from his grave, he would bring forth a terrible thunder and lightening to strike down all the ego-centered males in Asia who have used his name to hold women down for the past two thousand years.

As much as I love my fellow man, I still can't help feeling a certain fury about how intelligent men throughout the centuries, in the East as well as the West, have allowed ignorant men to hold women inferior.

• Protectors Abusing Their Power

In some fundamentalist militant Moslem cultures, women are considered just a little above dirt. Not long ago, the Moslem Religious' World Congress was held in Kuala Lumpur, Malaysia. There was only one female representative, Saleha Mohammed Ali

Bin Taib, and she was there to represent the Malaysian government. She is the director of the Malaysian Religious Board and the first Malay woman educated in England. In her address to the Moslem World Congress, she told a room full of holier-than-thou male religious leaders who were mostly from the Middle Eastern oil countries, "I am glad I am a Malay. If I lived in your countries, I would not be here today addressing you."

Kakak, which is what she prefers to be called, means "sister" in the Malay language. She told me that, although Moslem law allows a man to have four wives, in its original intent that law was created to take care of the livelihood of those women who had lost their husbands during the numerous wars fought at that time in that region.

However, it was turned into an instrument of gratification for the wealthy and lustful, thus making women the chattel of men. The intent may have been to protect, but the result is that men have abused their protective power. Those in control of our livelihood are in a position to abuse.

In the West, we have an equivalent situation in the relationship between some working husbands and non-working wives—the provider and protector abuses his protectees. From East to West, from ancient times to the present, the story has always been the same.

The essence of warfare is based on deception.
  —*Sun Tzu (1.21)*

It is women's obligation to see through the false basis of men's power. Heaven created this world with equality in mind. In the natural course of human evolution, the power of *yin* (the feminine) will swell and expand unstoppably like the waxing of the moon. What was kept down and humbled will surely rise high and be glorified.

This is the principle of *tao* and the universal righteousness. Anything against *tao* will seek its own destruction or correction.

Chin-Ning Chu

"The only time I've moved forward in my career is when I had the courage to say no to the things that were safe or that I'd done before, in order to create space for something new to enter."
—Helen Hunt, actor

NIKE SHOES, GLASS SLIPPERS AND COMBAT BOOTS

*A proficient woman warrior
always makes sure of success
before she takes on her challenges.
The loser is one who accepts her challenge
before she has any idea of how to obtain victory.*
—Sun Tzu (4.11)

It is against *tao* to blame gender inequality solely on men. Yes, they have definitely contributed their share to inflaming this evil, however, we women have also helped by lying to ourselves.

In today's business culture, we think something is wrong with anybody who doesn't want to get ahead. The assumption is that: of course everyone wants to get ahead! We are under such pressure to train our minds in a certain image of success that we suppress "unacceptable" thoughts before they even come into consciousness. We fear that by telling the truth about what we are, the lifestyle, dreams, and ambitions that we have so carefully cultivated may come crashing down. And so we go around unconsciously lying to ourselves, and pursuing what we *should* pursue by drowning ourselves with the noise of "noble" desires.

If you dig deep enough into yourself and have the courage to really find out what is right for you, like a life raft in the stormy sea, your honesty about who you are and what you want for your life will guide you to fulfill your personal happiness.

Some women are lucky enough to *know* what they want. They just want a certain level of comfort and a decent paycheck; they just want to be able to afford Nike shoes for their kids and no more. Such a woman without great ambitions is made to feel terribly guilty. So, even though she *knows* that she doesn't want to be CEO, she still has to grab for excuses to justify her lack of ambition. The glass ceiling is often one such excuse.

Then there is another type of woman who wants to get promoted, but she wears glass slippers. She has the ambition, she wants to be a warrior, she wants the executive office, she wants the fruits of a good life, but she doesn't have the warrior spirit. She wants success but is unable to give up her Cinderella attitude. Every woman has a pair of glass slippers she stores in her heart and there is nothing wrong with this. However, you cannot climb the corporate ladder with glass slippers on—for that you have to wear combat boots. It takes a warrior to climb the ladder. You have to outdo everyone else on your way up.

The problem is not with any of these choices. The point is that we need to choose: do we want the Nikes, the glass slippers, or the combat boots? Don't lie. Don't justify. Be proud of your choice. It is easy enough to find the external villains—there is no question that men have contributed to the suppressing of womanhood—but the major force keeping us in a state of vacillation is that we're not clear about what *we* want. Before we can move forward as a gender in this new century, we should take a sober look and see how we contribute to our own misery and our own uncertainty.

Why Is It So Hard For Women To Wear Combat Boots?

• We Place Fantasies above Reality

Once, during a conversation with a male bank manager in his office, he confided to me, "I would really like to promote capable females in this bank and nurture them, but as I look around I cannot find any qualified candidates." I looked around his bank and I could see why he was so frustrated. Right away I could see from the way these women presented themselves—the way they dressed, their body language, their verbal expressions and their outward attitudes—that these women did not take their careers seriously. Even though they were working in a conservative banking environment, most dressed as if they were school kids going to a class—some in long, flowery-print granny dresses, others in miniskirts with sloppy, lacy blouses.

To these women, it was more important to be sexy, young "chicks" and fulfill their girlish fantasies than to become tomorrow's female executives. The paradox is that you need to be powerful enough to be yourself and dress the way you enjoy expressing your particular unique personality, but you also have to obey the ground rules for your specific corporate culture. For the time being, every business environment has its special restrictions, and these are mostly set by men.

The point is, dress appropriately for your workplace and the position you aspire to. In another words, don't dress for what you are today—dress for what you want to become tomorrow.

Parenthetically, this rule of appropriate dress is not used to discriminate against women. In the business world, men must also wear a suit and tie if they want a key to the executive washroom, and they won't be accepted into the conservative corporate hierarchy if they insist on wearing a tee shirt with shorts.

Everything about us, from our clothes to our attitude to our skills, tells others what we think about ourselves and how we relate to our job. How can a woman expect to be promoted when she does not envision herself as a worthy candidate for advancement and expresses that attitude outwardly?

• We Lie to Ourselves about What We Want

It's perfectly alright to say, "I work to support myself and help out with my family income. I like my life and I want my son to have his Nike shoes." There is nothing wrong with a mother being content to work in order to bring in a little extra income. If that's your choice, you should be very proud that you are working to improve the quality of your family's life. It is a noble motivation—it is in line with *tao.*

If you acknowledge what you are really about—if what you really want is the Nike shoes—then you are a winner in your life. The glass ceiling will not apply to you because you are not one of the competitors who is attempting to climb up and shatter it.

Just as before you can take a journey, you must first determine where you are and where you're going, before you can do anything towards realizing your goals you first acknowledge where you are really at. Only then can you get where you want to go.

• We Wear Glass Slippers with Combat Fatigues

The most unhappy working woman is the one who enters the world of business, pretending to be a woman warrior, and yet deep down she is holding a Cinderella picture in her head. While she works, in her heart she is waiting for Prince Charming to come along and sweep her off her feet so she can *really* begin living her life.

So often, though, when Prince Charming finally comes and after the wedding, when real life sets in, she discovers that she has married a frog in disguise. She still must work and cannot have the life she envisioned—the golden castle with all its fine things.

Her heart is caught between her dream of being Cinderella and the internal need she has to gain recognition and advancement in the workplace. She may wear combat fatigues but, instead of combat boots she wears glass slippers—proving herself ineffective in both worlds. She is like a grudging warrior whose spirit is too weak to obtain victory while not having the luxury to surrender. Surrender—in this case walking off her job—is not an option for her. That is her economic reality. This is a story all too familiar to many working women.

Nothing is more lamentable than a grudging warrior trapped on the battlefield. She cannot go AWOL because her superior officer (her bank account!) will shoot her, nor does she have the courage to go forward.

You have to either throw away the glass slippers or the combat uniform. If you choose the combat uniform, wear the boots, too. The glass slippers go with the ball gown. Commit to your choice and have fun.

• We Buy into the Myth of the Glass Ceiling

For the real warrior who wishes to go up, it is not the glass ceiling but the myth of the glass ceiling that often stops her. The barrier of the glass ceiling is one of the major complaints I hear from corporate working women. It is very much like racial prejudice. It exists, but it does you no good to acknowledge its existence. Focus on what will benefit you—being excellent—instead of concentrating on that which will bring you down.

The corporate glass ceiling is like the emperor's new clothes: it can only be seen by those who are convinced of its reality. In a business dominated by men, the late Dawn Steel, president of Columbia Pictures, was the first woman to become president of a major movie studio. She started as a secretary and worked her way up the corporate ladder. When asked about the glass ceiling, she replied that she could not see the glass ceiling; it did not exist for her. It was not a part of her reality in her corporate ascension.

In fact, the majority of men in a position to promote women are not dumb; they know it is to their advantage to work with capable individuals regardless of their gender.

Recently I was invited by Helene Larivee, the general manager of Le Cirque Du Soleil, to see their performance. Le Cirque Du Soleil is by far the most artistic and entertaining circus on earth. Helene is in charge of the circus units touring the North American and Asian continents. I asked Helene, "The image of the circus is that it represents a macho, male-dominated world. Please tell me the single, most effective element that has contributed to your success in this environment?"

Helene, a delicate lady of just a little over five feet, replied, "I have always worked with men and I never felt that I was different from them."

Most women go to school with men and also work with men, but many of them feel they are being suppressed by men. Men become an obstacle to their career. Why? To determine the way in which you want others to see you, you must see yourself in that light first. If you don't like how others treat you, then change the way you perceive yourself.

Because Helene presents herself as a powerful, proficient businesswoman, men see her this way, too. They see her through her eyes, which are gender blind. The result is that she has no problem expressing how powerful she is in effecting her job with excellence in a business as tough as the circus world. All the successful women worldwide have one thing in common: they don't see the glass ceiling.

• We Lack a Powerful Spirit

It is not whether your words or actions are tough or gentle, it is the spirit behind your actions and words that announces your inner state. I once attended a party and the hostess told me that she was anxious to introduce me to a lady who worked as a trainer for the telephone company. The hostess told me that this woman was a powerful lady who was going to school all the time to better herself. Shortly after our conversation about her, the lady arrived. I was definitely not disappointed by the buildup. She was elegant, attractive and she dressed very professionally.

As I began to talk to her, I kept feeling something was incomplete about her but I could not put my finger on exactly what it was. Later she turned to speak to another girl whom she knew very well, telling her about a recent dream she had. I overheard bits and pieces of her dream. When she turned to speak with me again, I asked her to repeat the dream for me. For the purpose of this story I will call her Susan.

Susan had a mentor who was teaching commercial art. She was very fond of her mentor. In her dream, her teacher's husband had given her a piece of brick and asked her to throw it into a large glass wall. Susan found the request offensive. She *reluctantly* followed the instruction. She smashed the glass wall. Then her teacher's husband brought out a silver platter on which was placed a severed dog's head.

Susan had told me earlier that she consistently worked longer hours than anyone else at her company. Her boss always praised her for a job well done. However, whenever there was a promotion, he always passed her over. In order to try harder, she would take courses on weekends. She even took to wearing ties, white shirts and long pants to look like the men in order to compete. One couldn't say she didn't try. She was completely convinced that she was the victim of the glass ceiling.

After I heard her dream, I looked deeply into her eyes; all of a sudden, everything clicked. I found the "missing" element about her. Susan is from Georgia and, as a southern lady, she is very proper and had been brought up in the idea that a real girl should be "all girl."

In her dream, Susan's glass wall symbolized the glass ceiling. Her mentor's husband, symbolizing male power, instructed her to smash the glass wall (ceiling), which is against her elegant upbringing. So unladylike.

The severed dog's head symbolized the macho, male hunter instinct—very unfeminine, inappropriate and repulsive. Of course, a bloody dog's head is repulsive to anyone, but to her it was even more so. It went against every grain of her feminine soul to have her exposed to something so gross. The fact that the bloody dog's head was delivered by her teacher's husband symbolized that she needed to incorporate more masculine energy into her life.

Now I understood why I had felt no sense of power from her. Her dream revealed the missing link. Susan had even tried dressing like a man, but a mere tie and shirt could never cover the powerlessness in her soul.

On the contrary, when I first met Ms. Rafidah, the Malaysian Minister of International Trade, I thought the prime minister had to be out of his mind to appoint her to such a high position. She was dressed in a metallic, rainbow-colored Malay floor-length dress.

Her arms, neck and ears were decorated with gold ornaments and her eyes were painted bright blue. She looked like a walking Christmas tree.

However, as soon as she opened her mouth, her spirit shined through. Then, there was no doubt about it, she was powerful. When one is operating at this level of power, it doesn't matter whether she wears glass slippers or combat boots, that personal power shows.

The ultimate power is in our spirit. You can't fake it, you can't decorate it. You can enhance it by dressing well, but you can't fake it by dressing it up.

• We Exacerbate the Problem

Some authors have painstakingly compiled hundreds of pages of evidence that women are the victims in every facet of this male-dominated world. Because one of these books was so popular, I bought a copy. After flipping through the pages, I became so depressed that I had to stop reading.

If you didn't have an inferiority complex about being a woman before you started, by the time you finished this book you surely would. The reason for this book's popularity is that so many women would rather blame men for their lives not working rather than take charge of their lives under their own power and become winners.

However, books such as these, while making a convincing case, focus on the problem, but not the solution. Even though the book proved its case, the question still remains, "What will knowing all this do for me?" I already "suspected" that gender discrimination existed just as I "sort of" had some idea that when two trains came head-on at each other, the impact would cause great damage. But I would not spend much effort studying every detail of such a crash.

I'd rather spend my time focusing on subjects that will bring positive results.

Rather than moaning over being victims, it's time for women to transform ourselves into winners. To regain our inherent equality and innate superiority, whether our goals be that of the working woman executive aiming for the CEO's position or of being the lady of the house contributing to the joy of our family and the wellness of our society.

If you are convinced that you are not getting ahead because of your gender then you should do the following:

a. Find others whose judgment you trust and ask them to tell you why you are not promotable. In one of my workshops, a lady complained to me that her boss brought in outside people to fill the positions above her instead of promoting her. She was convinced that she was a victim of the glass ceiling. I brought her to the stage to have the group work with her. We could all clearly see that she needed a lot of work on her confidence, body language, and clarity in communication. The whole group could see that her problem was not the glass ceiling; it was her.

b. If after really searching the situation, you find that your boss is truly prejudiced against you because of your gender, then quit your job and find your destiny elsewhere. But, be sure to find a new job before you quit. It is a truism that it easier to find a job when you have a job. Employers like to hire people who are already working.

c. If you like your job and don't want to quit, then give one hundred and fifty percent to the job that you are doing. By doing this, a couple of things can happen. First, if you are really superior, you may stand a better chance of being promoted because it is in your boss's best interest to utilize you in a more effective way.

Or you may get fired because your boss is a real chicken-heart and he or she is afraid that you will take over their job. In this case, the universe has made the decision for you; it is time for you to move on to a better life elsewhere. Fear not, as long as your actions are in line with *tao* there is always a glorious destiny waiting for you.

Securing yourself against defeat
depends on your own effort.
—Sun Tzu (4.2)

From this moment on, we can dismiss the "glass ceiling" as an excuse forever. We are winners when we are content with our work and our position, whether it be prestigious or humble in the eyes of the masses. If you are happy with who you are, you are a winner. And that should be good enough for anyone.

Whenever I speak at women's conferences, some women tell me they are so happy that I "give them permission" to be a housewife who also works in the office. They confess that they have no desire to be CEO.

The world is large enough to hold dreams of different sizes and colors. No one dream is inherently better than the others; what counts is that you experience your life with ecstasy and fun. It does not matter if your prefer to wear glass slippers or combat boots, as long as your footwear is appropriate in serving your objective.

Of course, if you are a sharpshooter, like Ms. Rafidah, even glass slippers will do well in the battlefield. This is *tao*; this is your alignment with the will of Heaven and the goodness of humankind.

I can honestly say that I was never affected
by the question of success of an undertaking.
If I felt it was the right thing to do,
I was for it, regardless of the possible outcome.
                    —Golda Meir

MORE TAO, MORE SUCCESS

*Tao addresses the morality
and the righteousness of a battle.
This must be thoroughly understood
by those who would effect the outcome.*
—Sun Tzu (1.3)

How will you use *tao* in helping you meet your business objectives? From ancient times until now, all of the wise ones have urged putting goodness into life and business. Short term, immediate gains—be they personal or professional—often do not translate into long term advantages.

When one works against this simple principle, an ill fate awaits because the world is not purely physical, although scientists and businessmen like to simplify the matter. Yet, the reality of life is that this world is physical as well as magical. The more *tao* we possess, the happier we are, the more success we enjoy. As mentioned previously, by doing the right thing, you will always eventually turn in the right results.

Discover how much you are aligned with tao by asking:

• How Righteous Is My Objective?

Every situation has a "rightness" factor. In everything you do there is an integrity factor built into that task. If your cause is unrighteous and unsupportable, in time, defeat is certain. For this reason, Napoleon, Hitler, and all the aggressive tyrants of the world, no matter how brilliant they may have been, could not prevail for long. The same goes for the Taiwan builders who enjoyed short term success until *tao* caught up with them. What they did was against the will of Heaven.

If your objective is advancement, make sure you know why. Is it for the pay, for more profit, more recognition, more responsibility, more space for self-expression? More pay, higher business profits are all noble motivators that can ignite your desire to fight for your share. Nonetheless, unless you *fancy* your work for the sake of the work as the foundation for your desire for success, your motivation will not be sustainable in the long run. Otherwise, you may find when you are at the top—with power and money— you hate your job and yourself. In short, if you don't have a righteous objective, you will fail or make yourself terribly sick along the way.

On the other hand, when you do the right thing for the right reason, the right result awaits. When Joan left one of the major Fortune 100 companies for the newly formed company, she also left a million dollars retirement package. At the time she joined the new company she was not offered any partnership; she was only a hired hand. As she said to me, "It was the right thing to do, I traded a million dollars for a dream." Now this new company is considered the best managed, fastest growing company in the world. And Joan has been monetarily rewarded over ten times the million dollars that she gave up.

In today's swirling business world, things move so fast; you are never going to have enough data to make a "solid" decision. When in doubt, I ask a simple question: "Is this the right thing to do?" My golden rule is: "Do the right thing and the right results will follow." Sometimes the right result may be late or take a form that looks like the opposite of the desired result, but eventually it will be proven that *tao* will always save you and lead you to victory.

Even Joan, in the early years of the new company ran into some rough times and she thought she had made a mistake. But she said to me, "If the decision is the result of following undeniable inner guidance, how can that be wrong?"

• Is this Driven by My Super-sized Ego?

A super-sized ego holds the seeds of self-destruction. When Hitler waged war against the goodness of mankind, it was because he was blinded by his ego and was thinking that he was invincible and indestructible. Such super-egos contain blind spots. These blind spots exist at the soul or spirit level and it will lead one into making stupid decisions.

Alice, after having failed in her family business, was offered a directorship to run a paper-mill company. She told the chairman of the board that she would not take the job unless she was given a car and a chauffeur. After running the family business into the ground, she still didn't see that her own arrogance was her biggest enemy. What she should have done was to serve her employer, the stockholders and do a superior job. A car and a chauffeur should not be the focus of the job. She didn't get the job and, until now, she is still living off of her leftover, swiftly-diminishing family wealth.

• Am I Driven by Pure Greed?

If you're only in it for the money, you will fail. Confucius said, "A superior person understands righteousness, while an inept individual understands only profit." Whenever your motive moves from service to greed, wisdom to ignorance, you will pretty much know your motive is not supportable.

A five star hotel in Asia has a beautiful marble floor covering a lobby that is large enough to place an ice-skating rink in. This hotel, like all the other hotel lobbies, used to have a sofa, table and seats for the hotel guests to wait for and to greet their guests. The lobby was always full of people—like a night market—and business was good.

One day the hotel management started a construction project that blocked off the two square corners on both sides of the hotel entrance where the sofa and the chairs used to be. When completed, the management had turned the free seating areas into two coffee lounges. So now, if anyone wishes to sit in the lobby area, they have to buy coffee.

The coffee and tea are served at a price of nine U.S. dollars per cup and each additional refill cup for another nine dollars, plus the waiters constantly push sweets while you are sipping your coffee. A casual meeting of four people with tax and a service charge will run over one hundred dollars. The bottom line is, there are no free seats anywhere in this hotel. The obvious motive of the hotel management was to maximize its receivables. They did not have their guests' well-being in mind.

Bottom line profitability is the goal of every business, however, short term profit does not always translate into a sure winner. I was a frequent guest of this hotel. I found their new practice disturbing. I refuse to stay in this hotel and have now found another hotel in the city that is more user-friendly. I cannot support a hotel that will not allow me and my guest to sit in the lobby without charging me a toll fee.

Strange enough, three years after they put into practice their "no-free-seat" policy, they again installed an unencumbered small sofa and coffee table for their guests' use. I guess I was not the only one who hated the idea of being held hostage by the hotel management's greed!

• Am I Driven by Desperation?

You can file the word "desperation" along with the words "gloomy, discouragement, depression, fear, deprivation and hopelessness." The very feeling of desperation contains worry, anxiety, hunger, no-way-out, no-solutions, I-won't-make-it. All of these feelings cause *tao* to flee and you lose your power. Your mind will be paralyzed and cannot create outrageous and brilliant strategies. When you're in a desperate state, it is best to do nothing until you can let the negative emotion go so that harmony and hope and optimism—the characteristics of *tao*—can be restored. Otherwise, the more you act from desperation, the more you have to undo.

• Who Will Be Served and Who Will Be Hurt?

The more people you are serving on this planet and the fewer you are hurting, the greater will be your true success. Many large companies use all of their resources trying to figure out how to hook their customers with all kinds of fancy gimmicks; plus very small printed details of conditions that are almost impossible to read without a microscope.

However, in time, the consumers get smart and figure out which company is having their twenty thousand employees work on putting the screws to you versus the company that is working at serving you. Trying to "hook" people for profit will ultimately drive away customers. Providing a true and useful service to your fellow man is the only legitimate path to long-term success.

⚬

By asking the following questions
you will know which side will be the winner:
Compare the two commanders,
who possesses the Tao?
Compare the two commanders,
who is the superior individual?
Which side possesses the advantage
of timing and resources?
Which side possesses more discipline
and orderly executional procedures?
Which side has the more motivated staff
and possesses excellent equipment?
Which side has better trained workers?
Which side has a clearer standard
for reprimand and promotions?
                              —Sun Tzu (1.9)

By cheerfully aligning your objectives with *tao*, by doing the right thing, you are assured of having the right result follow. If you and your aim is in line with *tao*, then your success rate will most naturally increase. More *tao*, more success; guaranteed.

53

Chin-Ning Chu

II. TIEN—TIMING

Heaven is signified by Yin and Yang,
Manifested as summer and winter
and the changing of the four seasons.
—Sun Tzu (1.4)

Chin-Ning Chu

For what is done or learned
by one class of women becomes,
by virtue of their common womanhood,
the property of all women.
— Elizabeth Blackwell
(The first woman in the U.S.
to become a physician)

21ST CENTURY, THE WOMAN'S CENTURY

*The gushing water generates tremendous
momentum,
enough to float giant stones.
The flying eagle is able to destroy its prey
due to its precision coordination of distance and time.
A skillful warrior marches her troops into battle
by stirring up an overwhelming force of momentum.*
—Sun Tzu (5.9)

What is timing? In any given environment there exists a collective unconsciousness. Timing is the point at which unconscious awareness is pushing up into consciousness. There was a miraculous event that happened after the passing of December 31, 1999. We women became suddenly aware that we were tired of pretending to be men, that we wanted to integrate our fantasy feminine selves into our reality selves. We want to be more expressive as women, not only as working women.

This awareness was not clear in the collective female consciousness until the Spring of year 2000. Then you started to see evidence of it everywhere, a reflection of this deep yearning for a more feminine approach.

Even Saks Fifth Avenue's clothing ads for working women read, "It calls for an individual sense of style that is a bit adventurous; it's for those who welcome the new, the unusual, the unexpected; look at the world in a new way. Do something unexpected." The pictures showed young women wearing flowery or pinkish-colored suits, rather than the traditional men-inspired banker's uniform. This was a result of the shift in the unspoken collective unconscious.

Being in line with timing (*tien*) allows you to take advantage of the force of momentum, and momentum gives power. When you have timing with you, you are unstoppable. And that is what is happening to women as we enter the new millennium. We are moving from the Industrial Revolution to the Information Revolution, from his-story to her-story, from the Man's Century to the Woman's Century. Jump up and down and sideways—finally, the universal timing is with us. In this new century, this new millennium, woman will be the unstoppable force. "The 21st Century is the Woman's Century" is not just a slogan; we can easily turn it into reality.

Why the 21st century is the woman's century:

• Pacific Qualities Are Distinctly Female Qualities

The 21st century is commonly spoken of as the "Pacific Century" because the Pacific is, and will be, the leading growth area for the 21st century. Along with the rising of Pacific economic power will also come Pacific cultural values which tend more towards the intangible and intuitive.

We can identify the dominant themes of Western culture—direct, rational, logical, saying what's on your mind—as masculine qualities; the Pacific or Asian qualities are distinctly female qualities—intuitive, subtle, non-dualistic. Pacific culture recognizes a full spectrum of greys, that life is filled with ambiguities and paradox. That which is absent is more real than what is present—what you see, touch, and hear is less important than what you cannot.

From the late 20th century, Asian qualities have surfaced in the West—from Pokemon to the designer Vera Wang and the Disney cartoon movie *Mulan*. The movie *Charlie's Angels* includes an Asian angel; Stephen Covey's *Seven Habits* was full of Asian mental undertones; even James Clavell has edited a version of *Sun Tzu's Art of War*. These Eastern concepts would have been totally impossible to market in the middle of the 20th Century.

The corporate world is moving away from the pure material realm into the mental realm, and moving closer to Eastern thinking—the feminine aspect of the competitive force. However, this is only the tip of the iceberg; we will need a little more time to refine and complete this process.

• The Information Revolution Values the Unseen

Female qualities such as empathy, intuition, loving, being accommodating were considered inferior during the masculine-dominated industrial era. Now, as we move into the information age, muscle power is no longer the dominant force driving society; rather, brain power is where it's at. The innate female ability to discern fine shades of meaning and negotiate what is unseen will turn out to be the essential competitive tools for the upcoming century.

As we have mentioned before, the 19th and early 20th century approach to reality—the industrial model—was very muscular, very masculine, very matter-oriented. Now as we move deeper into the information revolution in the 21st century, our approach to reality is becoming more feminine, more Asian, more rooted in the innate female ability to grasp subtle matters.

• The Intersection of the Information Age and the Pacific Century Will Uplift Womanhood

The combination of the Information Age and the Pacific Century are on the skyline and will cause a great explosion in our awareness of feminine energy. This joint venture clearly signals that the new century will be the century in which masculine strength gives way to the subtler intuitive faculties that are capable of reaching and touching beyond the norm. Gradually, the 21st century will become dominated by this feminine energy. I can promise you that within the 21st century there *will be* a female American president. We have already seen major American corporations such as Hewlett-Packard and Lucent Technology promote a woman to the position of CEO.

• An Idea Whose Time Has Come

After all the reasoning, the best explanation is that the 21st Century is the Woman's Century simply because it is an idea whose time has come. In the southern California dessert there lies one of the largest boulders in the world; for millennia it stood forty feet high. From ancient times this Giant Rock had been held sacred by the native Americans; only the chief was allowed to go near and to communicate with the powerful spirit of this extraordinary rock.

It also carried an ancient prophesy passed down through the generations, the gist of which was that on a distant day in the future when this rock would come to split in two, this singular event would signal the start of the new Era of the Divine Feminine. On February 21, 2000, at 8:20 am, this Giant Rock did indeed split into half, exposing a white granite interior; as reported by High Desert Star newspaper—dateline Wednesday, February 23, 2000.

Among the five elements (gold, wood, water, fire, earth)
there is no eternal conqueror.
The four seasons rotate and make way for each other.
Just as daylight has long and short,
and the moon has waxing and waning.
        —Sun Tzu (6.26)

The fact that men have had political and economic power for the past few millennia is a function of *tien*, universal timing. But these same forces that put men in the ascendancy will also uplift women in the 21st century. There is no doubt about it, you can call the 21st century by its proper name: the Woman's Century. This is clearly due to the manifestation of the power inherent in universal timing.

21ST CENTURY, THE WOMAN'S CENTURY

We've chosen the path to equality;
don't let them turn us around.
> *—Geraldine Ferraro*
> *(The first woman Vice Presidential*
> *candidate of the United States)*

REMARKETING MAGNIFICENT WOMANHOOD

*The proficient woman warrior
will impose her will upon her opponents,
but she does not allow
her opponent's will to be imposed upon her.
—Sun Tzu (6.2)*

Anyone in the world of sales knows that all products need to be packaged and consequently marketed according to the image that they wish to portray to the world at large. This process is no longer limited to commercial goods but expands to include corporate images, from Whirlpool Corporation to General Motors, from the marketing of movie stars to the President of the United States.

By this logic, *Womanhood* is also a product—and surely the most mislabeled and misrepresented product of the 20th Century, if not from the beginning of human history. Womanhood has been marketed as inferior, unholy and castigated in terms of every miserable demeaning symbol mankind could dream up.

One example of such horrendous mislabeling is the myth that women are not suited to be professional fire fighters. Even I believed this until recently, when I received a phone call from a reader who happened to be a retired New York City fireman with forty years service. After he told me how much he enjoyed my books and how he has always supported women, I told him, "Even I think that a woman can do almost anything as good as a man, except firefighting. If I were trapped in a burning building, I would be very disappointed to see a female firefighter coming to my rescue. I would much prefer a great, hulking fireman to carry me out of the burning building."

My friend responded, "That attitude comes from the total fiction that has been portrayed in Hollywood films, showing a muscular man running into a burning building and hauling people out slumped over his shoulder. There is almost no way a single person can rescue anyone from a burning building. Because each of us are loaded down with so much heavy equipment, we always work in teams. If someone needs to be saved, it is done by a team effort.

"Furthermore, courage is not judged by gender. Women can be just as effective and courageous as any man in fighting fires. On the other hand, I have known a few male firefighters who were very frightened when facing a burning building. They are firemen because they have to support their families, but when it comes to a crisis situation, the rest of us cover for them."

After hearing a story like this, I'm sure we'd all like to apologize to those women who have dedicated their lives to fighting fierce fires. These women have had to tolerate the vicious prejudice of society and of some of their fellow firefighters. Misinformation about firewomen is fed by the images we see in film, and the filmmaking business, like most businesses, is dominated by the male gender. The obstacles facing the firewoman, and women in all fields, is part and parcel of the larger issue of the mismarketing of womanhood.

How can women take advantage of the opportunities to ride the waves of *tien*, timing? The power of timing will benefit womanhood in the 21st century in the same fashion that the full moon brings a high tide to lift ships stuck on a sandy beach. Just as the ship's captain needs to get busy steering the ship on its proper course, we women also must capture the universal timing and get busy repackaging and re-marketing womanhood to right all of the wrongs of the past, to sell the world a new image of womanhood.

How do we repackage womanhood? Easy, we just have to make something up that sounds appealing. All the mislabeling of womanhood was made up without any scientific basis anyhow. Now we can have fun making up something that glorifies us. I am sure that whatever we dream up will have much more truth in it than what has been made up before.

Here's what I made up about how womanhood should be marketed. However, I don't think it's particularly brilliant. I would like you to write to me and share your fabulous ideas about how womanhood should be marketed. Together, we can sell the world on a dynamic, new image of womanhood.

Womanhood should be re-marketed as:

• New Winners

In 1995, Mr. Koch, the industrial billionaire and 1992 America's Cup Winner, (America's Cup is the oldest sporting competition in history; it started back in 1851) put together the first all-women group to ever compete in the America's Cup, and everybody thought he was crazy! They said women are not strong enough, are not skilled enough as sailors, and are not smart enough to compete. The old guard in the yacht clubs just laughed and ridiculed. His all-women's team competed with the very best teams in the world, and they ended up in third place.

According to Mr. Koch, "If we had not made some fundamental mistakes, these women could have possibly won the America's Cup. The mistakes we made were that we did not have any women in our leadership. We managed these women as we would a bunch of males. We did not understand that women needed a different method of communication to be as competitive as they should have been.

"These women were incredibly strong. After training for about a year, they became so strong—so physically strong—that none of the men on the other teams would dare mess with them. At the end of the season each woman could bench press the weight of her significant other or the weight of her husband. We nicknamed one woman "the brick." She was five feet, four inches tall, two hundred ten pounds, had less than five percent body fat, and she could 'clean and jerk' her husband who weighed two hundred sixty-nine pounds.

"In fact, the first race that they entered, they dispelled all doubts that they were the weaker sex when Dennis Conners, the American yachtsman celebrity, challenged them and they [the women] won the race. Later, Dennis in a press conference stated that he would go down in history as having the two greatest defeats; one was that he lost to the Australians in '84 and two was that he was the first man to lose to a woman's team in the America's Cup. The women that were on our team were much tougher mentally and much tougher physically than the men were on the '92 team."

Women can win against men in every field. When we win we need to toot our own horns and let the world know that we are winners. We need to repackage and remarket the new winning image of womanhood.

• Great Team Players

The common belief is that men are better team players than women. Mr. Koch shared a very insightful story about how women can be even better team players than men:

"The other thing that we found when we were preparing for the America's Cup Race was that the women bonded together as a team within two weeks of being selected, whereas it took the men eighteen months and well into the finals before getting their act together.

"The women also got all the necessary chores done everyday. When we came in we would have to take the sails off, dry them out, clean the boat, sand the bottom, fix all the wenches, fix the mast— anything that had gone wrong. The women got all that done in less than half the time it took the men. The women organized themselves into very efficient groups. They wouldn't spend any time gossiping; they just got everything done whereas the men would say, 'Well, I'm too good to do that' and debate about how best to do the job.

"The women didn't want to be managed by what they saw as dictatorship. They wanted to manage by consensus, and we found that to be absolutely fascinating."

When I heard this, I was moved to tears by these women's tenderness and toughness as team players. Whoever said women are lousy team players obviously never saw these women in action.

• Effective Competitors

The common belief is that, because women are by nature more compassionate and sensitive to those around us, we neither want to compete nor are we very good at it. Mr. Koch remarks, "Our biggest mistake was that we should have encouraged the women to compete head-on with one another and also to accept leadership and exert leadership with one another. And I think that is one of the biggest mistakes in our society. Sports train our little boys to do this all the time, but they say little girls are not tough enough.

"Like the culture at large, the male coaches and managers perceived that the women would not want to compete with one another for positions on the team on the boat because they would not want to hurt their friends, but these women were as competitive and cut-throat in competition as any men we have ever seen."

Just because women are sensitive and empathetic does not mean that we don't enjoy the thrill of competition. It's a false assumption that one precludes the other.

• Creators and Bestowers of Beauty

Without women on the earth, civilization would look like a bachelor's pad—smelly, dirty, and messy. Legend has it that when President Kennedy was a senator, before he married Jackie, he rented a bachelor's pad in Washington. After his death, his landlord disclosed that his trash was piled knee-high. Here was this man who was so elegant on the outside, yet his apartment was absolutely filthy.

Women are the representatives of heavenly beauty here on earth. The beauty I speak of is the transcendent quality of beauty, not supermodel beauty. Supermodel beauty is set by fashion and trends. The world needs a feminine touch. Men can certainly have this feminine quality, but this beauty is woman's domain.

• Keepers of the Light of Humanity

From ancient times until now, men have been occupied with battles and wars, while women have minded the family and the home, providing the consistency necessary for humanity to exist. The light of humanity is expressed through woman's love, caring and harmony. Without these qualities, there is no illumination. Without the light of humanity there is no beauty to speak of. By ensuring harmony, love, beauty and happiness, women keep the light burning brightly.

• God's Police

There's a famous saying in Australia that women are God's police. Australian men are known for their ability to enjoy bar fights, drinking like fish, and getting rowdy just for the fun of it, so these lovable men credit women with keeping them in line. Men are always pushing the limits and boundaries for both good and mischief. It's easy to see that God made women to restrain men from going overboard. Imagine what men would do to each other and themselves if it weren't for women?

• Toughest and Most Durable

Our Maker gave woman the job of perpetuating the human race not by accident, but by design, because she is the tougher of the two genders. Women can endure much more pain than men, so the Creator gave them the most painful job—child delivery. Men would probably give up half way.

For thousands of years, when we didn't have the surgical procedure of cesarean section, babies were delivered by the sheer will of the mother, and many women gave their lives in the process of doing so. In everything we do, women's mental toughness and durability can make up for our sometimes lesser physical strength.

• Most Sensible

A woman carries her baby for nine months with loving tenderness. She cares for herself and for her unborn. She changes her life-style and deprives herself of numerous activities during her pregnancy.

If men had to carry the unborn, they would probably lose the baby during an "unavoidable" football match. This sensibility carries to how women take care of our families, to how we take the long view of our family's financial, physical, emotional survival. The preservation and regeneration of humanity is anchored in women's sensibility.

• Most Intuitive

That women can communicate with, care for and protect the defenseless infant is also by design, not by accident. By design, intuitive abilities are bred into women, ensuring the survival of their babies, and by extension, the species. I always tell my male executive clients that, when you are in doubt about your intuitive feeling concerning any incident, ask your wife's advice.

• Keepers of the Void and Guardians of Creation

In Asian philosophy, the Void is the space at the beginning of creation. Our Maker has created this space of void within each woman wherein the creation of life begins. This void is the incubator of human existence. Therefore, a woman is a microcosm of Creation and, on this planet, woman is the natural guardian of creation.

• Guardians of Mother Earth

There are three essential forces at work in the universe: destruction, creation, and the sustaining power. Men have thus far shown their immense talent for destruction, and, through their partnership, men and women create new life. But it is and always has been up to women to sustain and nurture life. Women put forth the necessary mental and physical energy that sustains the liveliness of their environment.

✍

The one who thoroughly understands
the advantage of adopting change and variation;
She is the superior commander.
　　　　　　　　　　　　—Sun Tzu (8.4)

Not long ago while I was in Malaysia, Ms. Rafidah, the Malaysian Minister of International Trade, told me a story. One question that the press like to ask of all women in powerful positions is: "How can you juggle the responsibilities of your demanding work and your family duties?" This question popped up yet again during a press interview held at the Singapore Airport.

　　Ms. Rafidah matter-of-factly replied, "Why don't you ask Lee Kuan Yew (the founding father of Singapore, their past Prime Minister and still the most powerful man in Singapore) how he juggles his office duties and his duty of being a father to his children and husband to his wife?" She continued, "This question does not deserve an answer." She then walked out, ending the press conference.

Repackaging and re-marketing womanhood is each woman's responsibility—especially in this dynamic new century. The universal timing is surely with us. But while the timing is right, we must take advantage of it. A high tide can lift a grounded ship, but without the good navigating skill of the captain you will have a runaway ship smashing itself up against the rocky cliff of the seashore. Just like that ship, each woman must do her part to actively embrace our new image as we aggressively market it to the world. If not for ourselves, then for all the generations to come.

Something which we think is impossible now
is not impossible in another decade.
> *—Constance Baker Motley*
> *(First black woman in the U.S.*
> *to become a Federal Judge)*

STEPS TO IMPROVE YOUR TIMING

*A proficient warrior seeks
Victory by employing opportune timing.
—Sun Tzu (5.18)*

Chin-Ning Chu

We all know, timing is everything, and yet timing is so uncontrollable. How can we improve our timing when there is no way to predict it? If, for instance, your product or service is ahead of the general public's taste, you will have a hard sell. If it hits the market too late, it misses the trend and all the sparks of innovation and freshness will have fled. You have to calculate if, from your planning stage to the time when your product hits the market, there will still be a void in the market that is waiting to be filled.

You cannot sell people anything they don't want; rather, your products must answer an unconscious longing within them. When they see it, they will realize they have been waiting for it. This is what Sun Tzu was referring to when he wrote of the "opportune timing" of the "proficient warrior."

How Can You Improve Your Timing?

1. Notice the Signals of Timing Hidden All Around

Timing is signified by the rotation of
yin and yang, winter and summer.
Favorable and unfavorable times.
—Sun Tzu (1.6)

During an interview Donna Karan was asked, "How do you determine what to design for the next season?" Her answer was disarmingly simple. She explained that she paid attention to the signals, large and small, all around her. Certain colors or designs

78

would appear and reappear over and over—on the street, in the subway or on television.

These signals let her know that she was on the right track and she would go with it. Every woman can relate to this. At one time or another, each one of us has utilized this "nonscientific" common sense process to help us in making decisions on when, how and whether to proceed with certain projects.

2. Be in Tune with the Timing of Those with Whom You Want to Do Business

In the morning, the spirit of the troops are fiery.
Towards the end of the day, they tend to slow down.
When dusk comes,
the men are thinking of returning to camp.
So, the skillful warrior, during battle,
avoids the enemy's high spirited moments
and attacks when the enemy is anxious
to return to camp.
—Sun Tzu (7.26)

People in the seminar promotion business know that timing is vital to the success of the seminar. If the seminar fee is to be paid by their company, the attendees prefer that the seminar be held during the business week. If it is to be paid by the individual, then the attendees prefer to have the seminar held on weekends. And, of course, one should avoid planning any seminars between Thanksgiving and New Year's Day or on major holidays.

If you are making a sales call or presenting a business proposal, it is best to avoid your customer's resistive period. For each situation and each individual this resistive period will be different.

It could be Monday morning, Friday afternoon or any other time of the week specific to the individual or business.

I know a magazine publisher whose most mellow time is after five-thirty pm when all the employees have left and all the office chaos has settled down. This is the best time to reach him. Of course, after five-thirty pm, the guard at his gate—his assistant— has gone home and he is left to answer his own phone. This principle applies just as well to scheduling a massage. Find out when the masseuse starts her shift and try to get an early appointment to take advantage of her best physical energy and attention.

3. Be Aware of the Relationship Between Your Objective and Timing

The good warrior's staging of an attack
is like the bending of the crossbow—
full of momentum and potential.
When she releases the trigger,
the arrow flies with a precise calculation
of distance, timing, and target.
Not too early,
not too late.

—Sun Tzu (5.12)

For the U.S. space program of year 2020, planning had to begin in 1997. It takes at least 20 years to implement all the new technologies, fine tune the problems, and launch a successful program. This means that planners had to have the telescopic vision to imagine what the space program could and should look like in 2020.

In order to be ready *and* relevant, you have to have good timing. When you're starting a new project or launching a new product, you need to answer the questions: how long will it take to complete the project and will it still be relevant?

There are no hard-and-fast rules here. Timing doesn't always mean being first to market. There are times when you might want your competitor to launch her product first, paying for the high cost of educating the consumer, distributors and retailers, then you can come in and ride the crest of the wave. You have to determine where your strengths lie.

If your strength is in R & D (research and development), then you have to be first to market. If you are best at cost controls and low pricing, then you want to follow the leaders and undercut their prices. The point is to align your objective with timing.

4. Use Your Intuition to Feel the Timing

Although people can see the execution of my tactics,
they are unable to penetrate the motives,
behind the creation of such peerless strategies.
—Sun Tzu (6.27)

Judith Regan, the publisher of the Regan Books at Harper Collins Publishers, once told me, "I stick my finger up and feel what the air is telling me about which book to buy."

Timing is closely associated with intuition, yet intuition happens spontaneously; by its nature it can't be planned. It's a gut feeling that can't necessarily be explained. Have you ever had the experience where you were discussing a topic with a group of people and kept surprising yourself with the pearls of wisdom that fell from your mouth, and yet when you got home you could not for the life of you recreate that state? Sometimes intuition can be stimulated by brainstorming, and thus, insight into right timing is suddenly revealed.

If we can tap our intuition it can certainly help us detect the rightness of our timing. There are many good books on fine tuning your intuition, but it's still a constant challenge to perfect that skill. In the meantime we have to deal with the inconsistencies and unreliability of our intuition. We need an additional safety net to help us verify the validity of our timing.

5. Back up Your Intuition with Data and Planning

The degree of success depends upon the extent of planning for anticipating victory:

1. Meticulous planning—Before engaging in battle, you have already won the war.
2. Careless planning—Before engaging in battle, you may have already lost the war.
3. No planning—Your defeat is certain.
4. Planning is the key to success and winning.
                                    —Sun Tzu (1.16)

Until you have perfect intuition you should plan on gathering solid data to back up your "suspicion" of what is proper timing. Guided by your intuition, at least you will have a healthy starting point instead of aimless wandering in ten thousand directions. Even if you do possess an infallible intuition, don't tell others that your source of information is rooted in your gut feeling. Let your gut feeling act as a compass to show you where to go to gather your data. Then go get it and be prepared to explain rationally how you arrived at your conclusions by solid planning and data gathering.

6. Use Common Sense

> *There is a proper season and time*
> *for utilizing fire to attack the enemy.*
> —*Sun Tzu (12.3)*

If the wind were blowing toward you, you would not set fire to the enemy camp. Always check which way the wind is blowing.

People enjoy barbecuing in the summer because the timing is with us. The weather is hot and dry. You wouldn't try to barbecue in a rainstorm. That's just common sense. Why work against yourself? Use your natural timing to enhance your objectives. The understanding of common sense is often not so common; it is a matter of understanding universal signals and timing.

Great timing (*tien*) is born out of the synchronicity between the surfacing of unconscious collective desires and the readiness of the perfect ideas/products/people to meet those desires. Timing is the gift of heaven. She often chooses to give her grace to those who are in line with rightness.

Even though we can't really control timing, we can improve it through detailed planning, incorporating intuition, using common sense and doing the hard work of gathering data, and then following up by executing our plan in a timely manner. By incorporating *tao* into our day-to-day lives we will naturally improve our timing.

Chin-Ning Chu

III. DI—EARTH

The earth contains far and near,
danger and ease,
open ground and narrow passes.
                    —Sun Tzu (1.5)

I've learned from experience
that the greater part of our happiness or misery
depends on our dispositions
and not on our circumstances.
                              —Martha Washington

TURNING LIABILITIES INTO ASSETS

Out of orderliness comes chaos.
Out of courage comes cowardice.
Out of strength comes weakness.
—Sun Tzu (5.14)

Nothing is purely positive or negative. It's all in how we use what we've got. In battle situations, certain conditions are fixed—there is a mountain in front of you, a river behind you—these factors you cannot change. Your terrain will always contain assets and liabilities; as a general in the battlefield your job is to figure out how to utilize and maximize what you have.

In life, it is as important to know your liabilities as it is to know your assets: to recognize how to turn liabilities into assets and be aware that what may seem like an asset is also a potential liability. For instance, to a large company, size can be an asset. There's strength and stability in size. But large companies are also slow to change, like elephants trying to turn over, and so size can also be a liability.

Li is a Major in the Chinese army, serving as a music officer. She applied to attend an elite battle training university numerous times and was rejected, even though she passed the rigid examination. All of the students accepted were male generals with battle experience.

After much resistance, the army finally granted her entrance to this special war college. My friend, a general who attended the same class with her, told me that every time they planned a battle, her strategy always beat the generals and that she consistently scored in the first or second position among the thirty generals.

The reason was that all the male generals had matriculated from the same military school and were all trained to strategize using the same classical postulates and methods. The lady major had never attended an official military academy and hadn't taken courses on battle strategy planning, so her thinking was outrageously different from the others in the class.

She was able to continuously provide surprises for her male counterparts. They had no idea what her next move would be and were always taken in by her unique solutions and arcane plotting. Being a woman and not from a traditional military school was her disadvantage, yet it turned out to work in her favor.

Being a woman can work for you or against you. Gender, like everything else in life, is neither purely positive nor negative. Everyone's life is filled with a certain number of liabilities. Yet, these so-called liabilities can be turned into our secret weapons for winning. Understanding how to turn our weaknesses into strengths, and exploiting our weaknesses for their inherent, hidden treasures can result in an endless variety of possibilities.

We can all turn our liabilities into assets by:

• Using All of What We Are

When one obtains victory,
by modifying her tactics,
in relation to her opponent's,
She is a divine warrior.
> —*Sun Tzu (6.32)*

Every woman is unique and different. Therefore there is no one answer to the question of how to use all of what you are. Some women can compete in a man's world and totally enjoy being a girl. If you are not afraid of being treated like a woman, you can enjoy men's chivalry and not be insulted by it. You can enjoy having a man open your doors and carry your luggage without feeling that your power has been diminished.

By being competitive, yet elegant; effective, yet gentle, you will confuse and fascinate and surprise your male co-workers and bosses. This can be a very magnetic quality. Men like to be around such powerful, yet mysterious and complex women. Being treated "like a woman" doesn't mean becoming a sexual *object*. Think of yourself as an equal professionally with the privilege of wearing silk stockings, high-heeled shoes and pink or lavender suits. This is the essence of Sun Tzu's statement above.

If you are an athletic woman, then use that to push yourself forward. No matter what type of woman you are, you can display your unique charm. What a thrill to watch the two magnificent women's teams compete in the World Cup in July 1999 in the Pasadena Rose Bowl. A billion viewers worldwide sat mesmerized in front of their television sets, watching the United States versus China in the Women's World Cup soccer game.

At the end of ninety minutes the score was 0 to 0. There was nothing more beautiful than watching these women compete. I was busy wiping tears and blowing my nose, moved by their gallant mental and physical commitment. Americans have never been great fans of soccer, so it was clearly not the soccer itself that interested American viewers; rather it was the playing of these vibrant women that captured the attention of the world.

This kind of girl power is a preview of what's coming in this new millennium. The very quality that was considered a liability—a wimpy, woman's sport—became an asset. And the world stopped and watched. Whatever your personal qualities—be they aggressive or genteel, elegant or sporty, collaborative or competitive—use all that you are to achieve your aims. A girl's gotta do what a girl's gotta do.

• Blossom Where You Were Planted

She wins her battles,
by making no mistakes.
The reason she can win battles,
without making mistakes,
is because she conquers,
an enemy that is already defeated.
            —Sun Tzu (4.10)

Embrace your life's every experience. Who we are, what we are, our birth, our upbringing—every moment of our life experience, be it joyful or sorrowful, is not wasted. Where you were planted, that is where you shall blossom.

Oprah Winfrey is the perfect example. Her phenomenal success as a talk show host grew directly out of the life she had lived. She was born into poverty, grew up surrounded by bigotry, got pregnant and lost her new baby at the age of fourteen. The very suffering she experienced in early life contributed to her sensitivity and enhanced her ability to relate to others. She blossomed where she was planted.

If you are a physically challenged individual, then within your handicap there lies hidden some very unique perceptions of which the common populace is deprived. The great educator and literary genius Helen Keller was born without eyesight, hearing or speech, yet, because she was not constantly distracted by the normal clamor of the senses, she was able to achieve a higher intellectual level than most people who posses all of their sensory faculties.

Physically challenged can never be considered an absolute road block to anyone's life. Only mental wimpiness and weakness can be considered the obstacles that prevent us from realizing our highest goals in life. Maureen Even, the President of Time Warner Trade Publishing, thrived and rose to the top in the very competitive world of book publishing in spite of the dual "handicaps" of being a women and having suffered polio as a child.

The kind of life we have is our Creator's way of preparing us to fulfill our personal and unique destiny. Life deals us all kinds of circumstances, some horrendous, like oddly formed building blocks in our life's mosaic. Until we start to work with these blocks, we cannot see the total picture; that all of them are essential to the composition of the singular and glorious portrait of our lives.

• Finding a Fresh Perspective

In a battle,
use your regular formations,
to engage the enemy.
Use unexpected surprises,
to overcome the enemy.
                                    —*Sun Tzu (5.5)*

It does not matter who you are, what you are, and what kind of product you are selling: be the first to explore and execute outrageous and unconventional strategies. The power of your strategy is embedded in its unfamiliarity; it takes others by surprise. Always seek the fresh angle, the unusual perspective in everything you do.

When you are looking for a fresh viewpoint, take a close look at the pile of physical and psychological garbage that has been labeled as your "liabilities," for there you may find buried treasure.

These liabilities are often overlooked by the majority of people. You may have a pretty good chance of finding a unique gem in there.

Daw Aung San Suu Kyi is a Nobel Peace Prize laureate and Burmese leader of the nonviolent movement for human rights and the restoration of democracy. She is an attractive woman who always wears feminine clothing and fresh flowers in her hair, circling behind her ear like a flower crown. By doing this, she is working against everyone's mental image of a revolutionary leader.

It is unheard of for a Burmese woman to be leading a revolution, and she thwarts our expectations of a revolutionary. Because she is a woman, a beautiful woman, the world has noticed her and has thus supported her cause. This one small woman is causing a lot of trouble for Burma's ruthless dictator.

Golda Meir, the past Prime Minister of Israel, often made tea and served cakes to her cabinet members and the foreign dignitaries who would come to her home for meetings. By acting like a cook and waitress instead of Prime Minister, by doing things that men would find unthinkable for a woman in her position, she disarmed the male ego. How can anyone be rude to a gracious grandmother-like figure?

Instead of waiting for someone else to blaze a new trail, search for new ways to market yourself and have the courage to manifest that thing that's so different from what anyone else has done. I can guarantee it will pay off in tangible benefits. But be careful, too: a good idea is only good if you can own and embody the spirit of the idea. Don't do anything just to be outrageous. It will definitely backfire on you.

• Understanding That Your So-called Liabilities Are Really Your Assets

Out of orderliness comes chaos.
Out of courage comes cowardice.
Out of strength comes weakness.
                    —Sun Tzu (5.14)

By the logic of what Sun Tzu has stated above, "Out of assets come liabilities." Our troubles start with how we define liabilities and assets. Liabilities are established by the majority in any given culture; but the same liability in one culture would be considered an asset in another.

The most important step we can take is to challenge what we have been taught to see as our liabilities, to not buy into the judgments of the mediocre (the majority) who make the rules. Every liability is a strength in disguise. Being a woman and an Asian in America would customarily be considered my weakness and liability. However, within this weakness, there lies the secret power of my personal strength.

Many Asians have said to me, "We heard the U.S. is a place that discriminates against Asians as well as women. You have two strikes against you. How do you handle this?"

My answer is, "Being Asian and a woman has proven to be my strength, not my weakness. If I were a blue-eyed, blond-haired male and had gone to the same public schools and learned the same things that everyone else in America had, I wouldn't know how to compete. It is tough to compete with people who are identical to you. To me, being different appears to be my liability but it is also where my unique strength lies."

Of course, if I were a blond-haired, blue-eyed male, I would have to find the things that make my life unique. Everyone has them. Being different is not your liability, it only makes you unique.

• On the Other Side of Your Strength Lies Your Liability

The universe contains five elements—
water, fire, wood, metal, earth.
Water can conquer fire, wood, and metal,
yet, earth can conquer water.
The same principle goes,
for fire, wood, metal and earth.
In each element's strength,
lies its weakness.

—Sun Tzu (6.32)

Just as your liabilities can become your assets, so can your assets contain potential liabilities. The circle of *yin* and *yang* is divided into half white and half black. Within the black half, there rests a white dot and within the white there rests a black dot. Within your liability, there lies your asset; and within your asset, there hides your liability.

If your strength is empathy and compassion, then you might also be prone to weakness and ineptitude when it comes to the disciplining your staff or your family. If you are very confident and quick to make decisions, you may also be intolerant and inflexible.

Be proud of your strength but don't forget to pay attention to how your strength may simultaneously be working against you. If you are keeping a watchful eye on your strength, you can make an adjustment and control your potential damage.

• Change Your Circumstance, So Your Liability Becomes Your Strength

Water finds its course according
to the shape of the ground.
The warrior achieves victory by devising strategies
according to the conditions of the enemy she is facing.
—Sun Tzu (6.30)

There's no point trying to fit a round peg into a square hole. If your job is as a creative artist, yet you are short on outrageous ideas and long in consistency and detailed accuracy, it is best you change jobs instead of trying to change you. Even if you could change you, it would be difficult to compete with those who are naturally outrageous.

Take a job as an accountant or logistical engineer and your past liabilities will instantly be transformed into strengths. Your new employer will be counting his blessings for having you in her department and you will be a much happier camper.

The purpose for learning the rules of strategy is to break all the rules, to create more innovative, even more unpredictable ways to overcome all of your competitors' predictability. The definitions of "strength" and "weakness" that come down to us from the majority culture are very one-dimensional.

We have to consider our personal attributes and life experiences and use them to turn our strengths and weaknesses upside down and inside out, to play with them. Only then can we turn our lives around and not be forever stuck with characteristics that we have no power to change. Understand how to manipulate the power of *di* as the expression of your brilliance at creativity and adaptability.

*I think the key for women
is to not set any limits.*

—Martina Navratilova

SWING YOUR BLUE MOMENTS INTO OPPORTUNITIES

*There are five dangerous faults that will
cause a general to fail:*

*When you are pledged to die, you are easily killed.
When you cling to life, you can be easily captured.
When you have a hot temper,
you will make regretful moves.
When you are attached to honor,
you can be easily shamed.
When you are over-prudent of your soldiers,
you fall victim to worry.*
—Sun Tzu (8:11)

99

Sun Tzu says that whatever we are, we can became a victim of that quality. One can safely say that the 20th Century will also be known as the "Perky Century." We have all become obsessed with this attitude of perkiness. If you are not perky all the time, people secretly think that there is something wrong with you.

But no one can be perky all the time. When we try to force ourselves to be, we set ourselves up for self-blame and self-criticism and a state of eternal unhappiness, because it is impossible to live up to such standards. In fact, I know many professional motivational authors and speakers and, when the spotlights go off, their lives are as miserable as everyone else's.

As Sun Tzu observed, those who are fearless of dying will make reckless moves which, in turn, will make them easy targets to be killed. Because of your unwillingness to betray your honor, you may thus lead your army into ruin. Whenever you take an extreme position, even for something as positive as trying to be upbeat, you can bring about your own discontentment.

Every quality is not purely good nor purely bad. Even good intentions can bring you bad consequences. As Sun Tzu's guru, Tai Gong Wong (who lived approximately one thousand years before Sun Tzu) said, *"Fragile has its value. Brutality has it place. Depression has it usage. Prowess has its aspects."*

According to Tai Gong Wong, every little detail of life, whether it appears to be positive or negative, holds the explosive power to transform your life and push you forward toward a better you. Allowing yourself to embrace those moments when you're not so perky has its definite purpose. Nothing in life is ever wasted; all you have to do is to know how to turn your everyday events—even your blue moments—into fantastic opportunities.

Swing your blue moments into opportunities by:

• Enjoying the Power of Simmering

Women's natural rhythms are more cyclical than men's. We go down into ourselves more often. Rather than fighting this, we should explore its positive aspect. Even the high jumper needs to bend down in order to jump. Nature contains and follows the cycles of change—spring, summer, fall and winter. In winter, the earth rests to have regrowth in spring.

The bear hibernates to rejuvenate for spring. Fortunately, the bear did not take a motivational training course; otherwise, with his new-found "wisdom," while the bear is trying to hibernate, he would be criticizing himself saying, "Get up, get up, you lazy bum." Part of his psyche would want to respond to the call of his natural rhythm of sleep, while the other part of his brain would be thinking about how he "should be" positive, perky, motivated, and get his butt up and going. When spring finally came, this poor bear would be extremely exhausted from his lack of proper rest. And we would have a very tired and cranky bear on our hands.

Human beings are part of the universal order of elements, and we are therefore subject to nature's fluctuations. Even water takes time to simmer before it boils. Without the power of simmering, there is no boiling water.

Simmering is not the same as doing nothing. Simmering allows you to gather power before an activity. It is part of your full spectrum of activities and creativity. Everyone of us has had the experience of becoming more dynamically productive after a period of simmering. I know that for myself, before a large project, such as the writing of a new book, I need time to vegetate. When I build up enough steam, I feel rejuvenated and the bottled inspiration feels like it is ready to burst. Then I can blast through the chapters in one sitting.

Everyone has a different simmering style. You might cuddle up in bed and read a book, watch television, play on the Internet, do gardening work, or cook up a feast that could feed an army. Give yourself the permission to just do nothing "productive." Simmering is a necessary part of the human cycle.

Enjoy, have fun. Rest, go inward; we all need to simmer from time to time. It gives us the strength to become boundlessly creative and wildly innovative. You may want to keep your simmering to yourself; don't let your co-workers and your boss know that your are simmering.

• Honor Your Blue Moments

Honor the blue moments. They are part of our creativity. Many of us feel inferior and shamed when our blue moments hit us. But as I have said many times before, every attribute in the universe has its purpose. If you are truly sick and clinically depressed, you should go see a doctor. But if you only occasionally feel low, it is important to honor your blue moments.

Women tend to be more aware of our low points. Men also have them, but they're not as in touch with them. When they feel low they find ways to stimulate themselves artificially to distract from the feeling—by going to their local watering hole and having few drinks or whatever. Winston Churchill called his blue moments his "black dog." However, his brilliance had a direct relationship to his "black dog." Without his blue moments, I am sure he would not have been half as brilliant a strategist and statesman.

The woman who must function in a man's world often feels inferior because of her natural emotional and physical cycles. Some men put women down when we are going through our physical cycles. If you're on your period, don't broadcast it. Keep your physical discomfort to yourself. Be kind to yourself. When we occasionally feel blue, keep quiet. It is nature's way of telling us we should slow down a bit. In solitude, we can regenerate our creative brilliance.

• Discontentment Is the Root of All Creativity

Creativity and innovation are rooted in the spirit's sense of discontent. By being discontented, the spirit searches for ways to improve its condition and a better channel for expressing itself. This sense of discontentment is the engine that drives all creativity and innovation. Bette Midler said her husband told her she was the most agonized person he ever met.

Jerry Seinfeld once said that he had to live in New York because the constant agitation and irritation of life in that city is the catalyst that creates great comedy. Of course, no one wants to live in agony all the time, but it's out of that grinding that the human spirit refines itself. Writers, artists, painters, architects, designers, poets, composers, comedians cannot create their extraordinarily brilliant artwork without it. Our blue moments are a necessary part of our human evolution.

• Accept the Cycles of Highs and Lows

Everyone in business knows about the cycles of sales. Even the best salesperson in the world has dry spells. The problem is that when she is going through these temporary cycles, her colleagues secretly judge her. Did she lose it? Can she do it again? The pain of knowing that others are judging you is far greater than your lack of income for that month.

Let me set the record straight: everyone has permission from me to have those low periods; this, too, is part of nature's cycle. During a Fortune 100 company's international retreat rewarding their top one thousand salespersons, as I was giving permission for the attendees to have a slow period, there was an audible, collective exhale of relief heard throughout the room. All of these top salespeople knew the secret pain of those uncooperative months of fluctuating performance.

The quicker you can accept your low performance month, the sooner you can bounce back. Blaming yourself and resisting your circumstances will only make you less effective. What you resist will persist. During the month of low productivity, take the opportunity to take that vacation to Europe, to Asia, to Alaska, to Florida. Just go somewhere to truly relax and completely forget about your work.

Changing your environment will help you to change your mental state, and that will unstick you mentally to bring you a fresh enthusiasm for work. If travel isn't in the cards, this is a great time to catch up on sleep, reading, gardening, taking care of projects around the house—all the little things you do to maintain your life. How we use our slow time has a direct impact on how effective we are during the hectic times.

∽

*To make the best
of your strengths and weaknesses,
is a question of the proper adoption
of the earth (geographic elements).*
—*Sun Tzu (11.37)*

When you set your life's objective to be a fun-loving winner, then everything you do is constantly acting towards that objective—including your setbacks, your blue moods, your ups and downs, and all of the significant and insignificant events in your life. All circumstances work together towards creating that rich, immense, multicolored tapestry we call a "winner."

The essence of *di* is to take what we cannot change and put it to work for our benefit.

Remember no one can make you feel inferior without your consent.

—Eleanor Roosevelt

CHANNELING THE RAGE OF SEXUAL HARASSMENT

When your force is in an inferior position,
move to defense;
when your force is superior,
move to offense.
—Sun Tzu (4.6)

**Sexual harassment—no matter how much you don't like it—is
virtually ubiquitous in our today's society.** No matter how many
laws we try to enforce to protect women in the workplace, as long
as men are wired to think about sex every seven seconds, we are in
trouble. There will always be some pitiful men who derive their
power from making vulgar sexual gestures or remarks.

"I can't think of a professional woman I know who has not
experienced some sort of sexual harassment," said Ellen, the vice-
president in charge of European, Middle East and African
operations for a Fortune 100 company. She continued, "When I
was going to the university and working for a large department
store, my boss, who had gotten to know me for period of time, said
to me, 'When did you discover your clitoris?' I went home and
cried that evening. I desperately needed the money to pay for
school. Here I was; working with a man who would say that to
me—I endured.

"I also think about the first time I joined a large corporation
after graduation from college. My general manager, during a
company meeting, stood in front of two-hundred-fifty engineers
and said, 'Now, I want to introduce Ellen. I am just delighted to
have her join us.' He went through my credentials. I thought to
myself, how wonderful that this man is taking the time to give me
a good start with this organization. I was sitting in the back; he then
said, 'Ellen, would you please stand to be acknowledged?' Again I
thought, what a wonderful way to join this organization. I was a bit
modest; I stood very quickly and sit down very quickly.

"He then pressed, 'Ellen, please stand up again. The fellows in
the front row didn't get to see why I am so pleased that you joined
our organization. She is one heck of a good-looking chick.'

"What he was saying in front of the two-hundred-fifty men was: '(1) She is a good-looking woman; (2) I am pleased that she is here because she is good-looking; and (3) I give the two-hundred-fifty of you permission to think of her in this way.' In those days we didn't have any kind of help regarding sexual humiliation. I simply filed it in the back of my head, 'Here is a man to watch out for.' In those days, women did not feel empowered to go after that behavior. Not that I would have legally; I tend not to solve things that way.

"I solve things by talking to the person now. I can tell you probably at least fifteen stories about me; what I have endured while coming up in my career. I will tell you though, interestingly enough, when I started to move up to the director and vice-president levels, these kind of things stopped. When a woman gets to a certain level, men know not to mess with her because she will come after them. Men are more sensitive about this issue now."

I asked Ellen, "When you said that you tended to not take legal action, that you talk to the man, what do you say?"

Ellen replied, "I try to explain to him that kind of behavior creates issues for me and, if he is doing this to other women, it will create issues for those women also. I tell him he is lucky that I am not a litigious-minded person and that there are women who would see this as an opportunity, not to educate, but to litigate. I am coming to him from the standpoint of: (1) Don't do this to me; (2) You're putting yourself at a great risk with other women; (3) As a senior person in this organization, your job is to set an example.

"I reflected about the early days in my career. That kind of discussion would not have happened because I was the one down the ladder. I was young and new to the organization; I had not established the credibility as this person who behaved this way.

"I remember a chronic and difficult situation for me that I endured for two years. Once I built my credibility and a support system, I dealt with it. Women who are not in that place probably endure and chip away a little at that time.

"I think sexual harassment does damage to women. I am one of the six women who has attained my level and position in my company. People will look at me and say, 'She is powerful; she is successful in this male-dominated engineering company.'

"But I would also say that I have a place in my heart which is full of anger. The anger is about the years and years of endurance, and knowing that, in order to preserve oneself in the workplace, you cannot be a litigious woman, but a woman who endures. In the end, the endurance has allowed me to achieve what I hoped to achieve."

Ellen's experience is common among working women. She obviously handled herself very well in her career progression by enduring the pain. Ellen didn't let the experience destroy her, rather she tapped into the experience and moved herself upward, in order to be in the position to do something about it.

How to handle sexual harassment:

• Use the Anger You Feel to Fuel Your Advancement

Ellen agreed with me that her anger had also become the force that moved her career forward and upward. By going through the humiliation of having to endure, she became a better support system for others who had encountered this pain.

Finally, Ellen concluded sharing her feelings with, "There is something that has helped me with my anger. I don't believe men get up in the morning thinking, 'I am going to make a conscious effort to sexually harass this woman, or cause this woman to feel less than others in the workplace, or ignore this woman.' I think they are the product of our culture. Until it is pointed out to them, they will continue to do it. I believe ninety-percent of the men are not evil."

Sexual harassment diminishes the person who is doing the harassing, not you. It can only strengthen you. I feel sorry for the man who must harass women in order to feel secure about his manhood, because, with each vulgar sexual gesture or remark he delivers, it diminishes him and acts as an acid to burn away, piece by piece, the virtue within him. He is just exacerbating his machismo and stupidity. Sexual harassment diminishes the person who is doing the harassing, not you.

• Keep Good Records

After a three day workshop in Australia, a lady came to me. She was crying profusely and thanked me for my book which had supported her through her ordeal. I held her tightly, but I was clueless about what had happened. After all the hugs and kisses with the other five hundred attendees were finished, she told me her story in private. She was fighting one of the largest companies in Australia for sexual harassment. Her problem was so severe that she had contracted terrible headaches.

After an exhausting year of fighting, she won her case. The reason she even had a chance at winning was that she had kept very detailed records, the specific details of harassment with dates and times. Along with this, she could also show by her medical records that, whenever she was harassed, she would have terrible physical problems. Without her records, she would never have had a chance.

Even if you don't choose to sue anyone, you should always keep very good records. You will never know when they may come in handy.

• Strengthen Your Esteem

Sexual harassment intrudes upon your physical and mental privacy. You can go to the authorities to report your case. You do have a lot of rights and are protected by law, but sometimes, even if you win the case, you lose. Both men and women employers will fear you and keep you at arm's length. Colleagues may applaud you for your courage privately, but knowing you are trigger happy, people may tend to stay at a respectful distance. Furthermore, even if you put forth your utmost effort, you may still lose the case.

Not long ago I read in a Taiwanese newspaper about a woman attorney who works in the office of the Supreme Court. She couldn't stand her male colleague's verbal sexual assaults at the office, so she filed complaints and lawsuits. The result was that the man was fined approximately forty US dollars and she lost her job. Stories like this make your blood boil.

Sexual harassment is offensive, but it cannot diminish or damage your self-esteem. If our esteem were so frail, then we would have a serious problem. You must be careful, in our lawsuit-happy country, fifty percent of the attorneys are frantically looking for new cases, and will brainwash you, once you have been harassed, into thinking that you are damaged psychologically. If you don't feel damaged, the attorney will certainly convince you that you should feel diminished for life. It may just turn out that your friendly attorney and protector might do worse damage to you than your initial offender.

If it is to your best interest, avoid direct confrontation, but protect your inner esteem.

One who is skilled in defense hides
beneath the ninth level of earth;
one who is skilled in offense travels
above the ninth level of heaven.
Such a person can protect herself from harm,
as well as obtain a speedy victory.
—Sun Tzu (4.7)

As a great Chinese philosopher once said, "When the universe intends to glorify an individual, she must first go through extraordinary hardship in body, mind and spirit. Then she will be ready to take on the great task." Instead of getting crushed, explore the possible silver lining in each dark cloud. When there is the lack of a perfect, ideal solution to this obnoxious problem, besides seeking support from your sympathetic family and friends, the best weapon you can have is to be very strong within yourself.

This is the exercise of *di*. Sexual harassment cannot damage your self-esteem. You are mightier than your unfortunate circumstances and your small-minded harasser.

*I abide where there is
a fight against wrong.*
                    —Mother Jones

CONVERTING SEXUALITY INTO ADVANTAGES

*Possessing the ability to calculate the difficulties,
danger, and distance is a basic requirement
for a good general.
A great general should know how to utilize
the natural lay of the land,
for this is a soldier's best ally;
but nothing is as decisive for victory
as the ability to read your opponent.
—Sun Tzu (10.16)*

115

Women are always willing to talk about how our sexuality has hindered us in the world of business. We are even willing to confront the painful experience of sexual harassment. But when it comes to discussing how we use our sexuality as a competitive edge, we keep our collective mouths shut. How each one of us may use our sexuality as business tool is a very private matter. I think it is okay not to let men know how we use our femininity to our advantage, as long as we are willing to tell the truth to ourselves that being a woman has its hidden assets.

Being the daughters of Venus, we have inherited her beauty, sexuality and sensuality. If our sexuality has brought us unwanted harassment, then we need to turn our sexuality into our advantage. Sexuality is not sex; it is attitude. It is the expression of the inner beauty of being a woman.

You can convert your sexuality into your competitive advantage by:

• Using Your Feminine Charm to Get Men to Work Towards Your Objectives

Being a woman, you cannot separate yourself from your natural feminine charm. I can't tell you exactly what feminine charm is because each woman's charm is unique. But, we all know that particular charm is a property of womanhood, and it is definitely different from a man's charm.

You must not fear exploring how sexuality plays a role in your working life. Whether you want it to or not, your sexuality will play a role (at the very least subconsciously) for or against you. You have the choice of whether you will be the master of that energy or its victim.

As little girls, we all know how we used our sexuality to manipulate our father and brothers to gain certain advantages. A daughter knows how to give that look through the corner of her eye that will melt her daddy's heart. By the time we are teenagers, women intuitively know how a boy's big head follows his little head. We use this power to get the boys to do us favors large or small—from getting you a glass of soda to doing your homework.

At home, your sexuality can direct your man to do things he does not like to do, such as washing dishes or taking out the garbage. The workplace is merely the extension of home life. Use your sexuality (I'm not talking about *sex* here but sexual energy, charm, appeal) to motivate your male co-workers, bosses and clients to accomplish your objectives.

• Attract New Clients with Your Sexuality

Recently I saw a television report/interview on MSNBC with an attractive young female attorney specializing in banking that was having a hard time getting in to pitch her services to her high profile potential clients. She placed an ad in an influential business banking magazine to solicit more business.

She said that, because 90% of her potential clients were men, rather than create just another boring business ad that would get no response, she put in a picture of herself wearing a suit jacket, miniskirt and super high heels. She stood tall and powerful, with her legs open, one foot up on a chair. The young attorney said that, as a result of this ad, she had gained many powerful bankers as her clients. The ads got her in the door were she was then afforded the opportunity to demonstrate to her clients just how good she was at her job. This story is unbelievable, but true. By the way; it caused her male competitors to cry, "Unfair advantage!" for her use of assets that they didn't possess.

• Use Your Feminine Power to Remove Barriers and Resistance

During my lunch with Amy, a high powered sales rep for an industrial heavy equipment company, she said, "It is good that men are driven by their sexual interest. We are all sexual beings. If you know how to use the power, it is not so horrible. It keeps potential male clients wanting to spend time with you and listen to your presentation and persuasion."

Amy continued, "Just as when Elizabeth Taylor helped her then-husband John Warner campaign for congress a few years ago. Liz said, 'People come to see me, but they get to hear John's message. So they get to vote for him.' As Liz uses her fame, and sexual charm to help her husband, I use my femininity to remove the barrier of resistance."

More women have used their femininity to remove barriers than we are willing to admit.

• Zig-zagging Your Way Up

We can all learn something from Gretchin. In the 1990s she was the only female who had ever been promoted to general manager at this very conservative Fortune 100 company. This mid-western company was so conservative, they encouraged their employees of both sexes to wear a corporate uniform standard of clothing—for the women: no tight-fitting dresses, no tailoring, no form, no flashy colors. When you entered their factories it was like going into a Puritan church.

But not Gretchin. This six-feet tall German beauty always came to work in three-inch high heels and fitted suits. She wore her clothes with such an ease. Though she was stunning, her wardrobe did not give the impression that she was trying to display herself. During meetings, she would listen to others while she used her right hand to lightly caress her neck where it was exposed just over her suit collar. When she got up to make a speech, she would take a deep breath and unconsciously expand her ample chest.

All the men in the company were drooling over her. All the women envied her for her beauty and her courage to flaunt it. Gretchin's career zig-zagged all the way up. Gretchin was very aware of the power she held over men and she used it well. But every man knew—from the board members to the stock boys— Gretchin was not available to anyone except her husband.

• Include Your Sexuality as a Part of Your Résumé

Rose is an attractive girl who used to work for minimum wage in a department store as a sales clerk. A year ago she got a new job promoting the famous wonder drug Viagra to doctors, so that the doctors would not forget to write prescriptions for their patients. Such a job normally requires one to have a pharmacist license, but she had no pharmaceutical background.

The drug manufacturing company recognized her feminine resources as a greater asset than her liability due to her lack of medical knowledge. As the majority of doctors are male, her look and her friendly personality would usually suffice to entice them to receive her. The biggest challenge for a pharmaceutical company is to get the physicians to be willing to speak to their sales reps during the doctors' extremely busy and demanding schedules. The company hired her and sent her to a three month long intensive training course. The result is that the doctors enjoy her visits and her sales record is exemplary.

Not every girl can have a killer body and an angelic face, but each one of us has something that is unique and attractive. Accent that. Use it to help you move forward in life and the workplace.

• Tap into the Energy of Anticipation

In business, if you flaunt your sexuality without keeping your feminine dignity, you might easily screw your way to the bottom—always a bad career move.

Never dish it out; the anticipation of the feast in a fine restaurant is always better than the feeling you have after stuffing yourself and being presented with the bill. As long as he is fantasizing about his expectation and anticipation of the feast, he will keep coming and hanging around for your command. Just don't send out an irreversible, mistaken message that can cause you great harm. Make sure you don't go so far out that, when you pull out of the game, he feels deceived.

• Be Sexually Powerful at Any Age

Sexuality is not the proprietary property of the young and beautiful. All of us can recall someone we know who, even at the age of sixty, through her smile or with a special gaze, could melt our hearts. We just want to do something nice for her.

*She who knows these strategies,
will win.*

—*Sun Tzu (10.17)*

I am sure, some militant feminist book reviewers will blast me for setting the feminine movement back fifty years, but I am just being realistic. Life is not laid out nicely and all politically correct.

As long as men remain fascinated by female sexuality, women will have to find ways to convert their power of sexuality to their advantage. This is the innovative way to utilize *di*. Incorporating your sexuality does not require you to do anything. All you need do is to simply be aware of the power of your womanly charm.

Without emotion there is no beauty.
You don't have to be born beautiful
to be wildly attractive.

                    —*Diana Vreeland*

PUTTING YOUR OWN SPIN ON STYLE AND SUBSTANCE

*The struggle for survival
will give birth to a new force.*
—Sun Tzu (11.61)

In our attempt to win the social and economic battles, women have found the new force of combining substance with style— an unbeatable combination. In the workplace, substance is essential, but career success is not solely dependent on substance; it is also about perception. You may really enjoy dressing like a Raggedy Ann doll with mismatched clothes covering your body as a statement of feminist self-expression, but don't forget that, for the time being, you are still living in a man's world.

You will have problems accomplishing your career objectives if your boss or clients cannot get past your appearance. Without good packaging, nobody will ever get to know the worth of the product. Life is pageantry, and the spirit of pageantry is in the beauty of formalities.

A news commentator once spoke of the presidential race between Walter Mondale and Ronald Reagan as a battle of substance versus style. Mondale had the substance, Reagan had the style; and style won. Reagan *looked* more presidential, so he got the job.

It is my non-scientific observation that most working women possess more substance than style, myself included. The good news is that it's easier to acquire style than substance. This is why television fashion make-over shows are so popular; any woman can get an instant transformation with proper tutoring. Substance, on the other hand, must be worked at just as one labors over the contents of a book. It is much easier to create a book's cover than to compose the substance of a book. Since the rest of this book is focused on growing your substance, in this chapter I will focus on how important it is to cultivate an enchanting style.

There are no ugly women, only lazy women. The first step towards enhancing our style is the awareness that good health is the foundation of style. I can't stress enough the importance of eating right, exercising and taking good care of yourself. There are so many books and articles written about this subject, and you know exactly what to do.

The question is whether you think feeling great is something that is important to you. When you are young, you don't feel bad enough to care; when you get old, you start to feel not-so-good, and you start to do catchup work. If you take care of yourself when you are young, when you reach fifty you will look not a day older than thirty-eight. This is called "growing older with style and elegance."

Just what exactly is style? The famous Italian designer, Valentino once said: "If you have good attitude, you have style." Others think style is a form of discipline. Style is the preview of who you are.

Style is not only about the way you dress; style is about your attitude, your facial expressions, your body language. Basically, it is the impression you give about you as a person. You do not have to be born beautiful and a size six to be stylish. Your style projects who you are and where you are going. To me, style is like the packaging for a product—your substance is your product, your style is the product's packaging. Both are equally important in representing the product.

I cannot really tell you what is the right style for you. Betsey Johnson's style is unique, so unique that she became a successful fashion designer. Many will think she looks like someone who came out of the nut-house, while others love her sense of style and fun. However, if you are working in a conservative male-dominated environment, (for the time being, maybe things will change in the future) you need to suppress your urge to dress like Betsey Johnson—unless you own the company.

Finding the style that fits your state of life takes some experimenting, and that can be very costly. Fashion consultants and image makers are not foolproof. You have to pay for the clothes plus their fee. Doing it yourself, can be costly in time and you may end up with a closet full of mistakes.

Develop an artistic eye by doing more studying, reading, shopping, experimenting and buying less. However, being stylish does not mean being a fashion victim by following the trends aimlessly. Hopefully, while in search of what looks good for you, this experience also provides you a little feminine fun as well.

Whatever you must do to find your style, find it, because style will certainly always play an important role in our life.

To make your style earn for you:

• Use Style as Your Resource

A Chinese proverb says, "Humans depend on clothing to stylize them, as the statue of Buddha depends on gold ornaments to glorify it." This statement holds more truth for women than for men. The movie *My Fair Lady* is a testimonial to how, with the right clothes and manners, a commoner can be transformed into a princess. The story of Cinderella again shows that style can really make the girl.

It is not by accident that both of these popular tales have as their central transformational characters, women, and not men. As much as style is important to a man, it still does not have the dramatic effect on men as it has upon women. All else being equal, style is the most dynamic and effective weapon that can be brought in for transforming a woman. I know it is extremely time and energy consuming to improve and refine your personal style, but just think about the possible rewards.

• Change Your Style, Change Your Career

Jane Pauley was fired from her NBC morning show job because she was getting too old. The network decided they wanted a younger woman to do the show. Years later, after Ms. Pauley had changed her hair, her wardrobe strategy, and had a complete style makeover, she became the host of her own show, *Dateline,* and made a comeback to become stronger than she had ever been.

Diana Vreeland, the arbiter of American fashion in the 20th Century, was offered a job by Harper's Bazaar as fashion editor because the chief editor, Carmel Snow, saw Diana's vibrant style while she was dancing with her husband on the rooftop of the New York City St. Regis Hotel. At the time, she was a housewife and pressed for money to help supplement her husband's salary. Eventually, she became her family's chief breadwinner and the editor-in-chief of Vogue magazine.

• Let Your Style Speak for You

Arielle Ford is the publicist who is responsible for making some very high profile authors famous. Once, during a lecture, she said that when an author appears on television it is not what she says that sells books; instead, it totally depends on whether the audience likes her or not.

It is common knowledge that during a job interview, the decision is made by the interviewer during the first thirty seconds. Style speaks for you and about you before you ever open your mouth.

• Improve Your Style, Increase Your Income

Consider Madeleine Albright—as her career progressed, she must have had a style consultant's help to pull herself together. After she became the Secretary of State during the Clinton administration, she used more (much more) makeup. I remember when she was previously serving as the U. S. ambassador to the United Nations. Occasionally she was unexpectedly filmed during a U.N. meeting, and she often looked as if she had just rolled out of bed.

Even Senator Hillary Clinton had to work on her style during her senatorial campaign. It was obvious that she had put a great deal of effort into trying to improve her packaging As First Lady, she used to look like a little Raggedy Ann doll; like she had just thrown something—or anything—on herself that morning.. Her lack of style in the early days of her husband's presidency directly cost her approval points. And it is certain that she will continue to improve her style until she becomes the first female President of the United States.

Nancy Reagan, on the other hand, had nothing but style and the American people approved of her. There were beltway rumors that she was the evil witch of the white house; that she would borrow clothes from famous designers and then conveniently not return them. None of these vicious rumors ever hurt her because she was pleasant to look at—she had style. Jacqueline Kennedy Onassis, having an abundance of both substance and style, was raised to legendary stature. Even her questionably controversial marriage to Ari Onassis did not hurt her.

While other people send their old clothes to the Salvation Army, the late Diana, Princess of Wales, raised 3.6 million dollars for the Cancer Society with her old wardrobe. All this occurred because she had dedicated her life to creating such a dynamic style for herself. Anything she had, we wanted a part of it. Yes, she was a princess, but Fergie was a princess also. The title alone didn't do it; it was the person who projected that elegant style who we liked.

While Diana was cleaning up her closet, Fergie was also, but no one wanted Fergie's clothes. The popularity difference between the two princesses was like the distance between heaven and earth. It was not only because one was the wife of the future king; it was because one had astronomical style and substance and the other was most certainly short on style (although Fergie has improved greatly in the intervening years).

If it is to your advantage to make a move,
then, by all means, move.
If it is not, stay put.

—*Sun Tzu (12.19)*

Style may be mystical and hard to define, but it will always pay the bills for those who are smart enough to cultivate and possess it. Princess Diana fit the image of a princess; her beauty and style still enchants us all and she will live on in legend for perpetuity. Actor Ronald Reagan fit the image of the President, so we gave him the job.

It is important to create a style that will intensify our professional savvy and magnify our personal charm, just as an actress' wardrobe can heighten the part she plays. Don't dress for your current position; dress for the role you want to obtain. When you look the part, most likely you will get the part. Enjoy this makeover process by becoming wildly innovative with the fashion trends and style, rapidly adaptive to the clothes you already have in your closet, and brilliantly creative with your personal statement of style.

Chin-Ning Chu

The ideal union between the sexes
shall result in the highest
development of the race.
—Susan B. Anthony

UTILIZING FEMININE AND MASCULINE ENERGIES

Proper adoption of the masculine strength
and the feminine softness,
is about understanding how to use di.
—Sun Tzu (11.37)

Recently, during a large business conference, I was the only female to speak along with a group if six noted male luminaries: Ex-President Jerry Ford, Prime Minister John Major of England, Congressmen Jack Kemp and Bill Bradley, television political commentator George Will, and star football quarterback Terry Bradshaw.

During my forty-five minute segment I mentioned that the perfect human being is one who possesses fifty percent male and fifty percent female qualities. In order to be effective in the world, a woman needs some masculine qualities. Unless her objective is to become Marilyn Monroe, a total sex symbol, she should not be totally feminine. By the same token a man who adopts feminine qualities will be a better boss, a better businessman, and a better father and husband.

This statement took only thirty seconds to deliver, yet, by the end of the conference, the attendees had singled it out and were engaging in a heated debate over the concept. Women reacted with emotional exhilaration and, while some men loved it, others were offended by the idea that the best men incorporate fifty percent of the feminine. Those men who hated the idea were surely in need of a good dose of feminine qualities!

Every great boss, worker, wife or mother has a balance of feminine and masculine energies; this also goes for great beauties. Two hundred years ago the French government gave the United States the Statute of Liberty as a realized symbol of the immense vitality, strength and beauty of our new nation. No one can deny her feminine beauty, yet, while she illuminates for us the epitome of Woman's loveliness, her face also shamelessly exhibits her inner masculine strength and determination.

The world considers Michelangelo's statue of David to be an inspired representation of the highest perfection in Man. But, as the artist carved masculine strength into each fiber of David's body, he also installed a feminine sensitivity into the soul of his David statute.

A certain sect of Chinese Buddhists preach that only an inferior soul takes birth as a woman. Upon hearing my Chinese girlfriend, with a serious face, tell me that all inferior souls are born as women, I was ready to toss my lunch from disgust towards all the ignorant ones who believe such a ridiculous doctrine.

The greatest deity in the Chinese Buddhist tradition, Guan-yin, the Mother of Mercy, is a woman. You see her beautiful statue or painting in many fine hotel lobbies or museums world-wide. In order to justify that the Mother of Mercy is not an inferior soul, Chinese Buddhists had to weave the ridiculous story that Guan-yin is not a woman.

They decided She is actually half man and half woman. This was told to me during my visit to an ancient Chinese temple. I wondered if her top half or her bottom half was masculine, or should we cut her lengthwise?

When humans want to believe something, they will find ingenious ways to justify it. The true spiritual meaning behind the concept of Guan-yin being half man and half woman is that she possesses the perfect balance of both male and female qualities within her.

• The List

One day, on a whim while I was giving an all-woman seminar, I decided to have the attendees shout out from the audience the various attributes that they thought were dominant in each of the sexes.

With the help of the workshop participants, I compiled a list of men's and women's positive and negative qualities. Bear in mind that this list is definitely NOT scientific and is seen from a totally subjective female perspective. You will see the humor in how we women see men, and how we see ourselves.

Although the list has no basis other than how we felt at the time, it has a gut-level honesty that's worth paying attention to.

MEN'S NEGATIVE QUALITIES:

Arrogant	Lazy
B.S.-er	Lecherous
Bad communicators	Liar
Brag about sexual encounters	Macho
Bulldozer	Male Chauvinist Pig
Childish	Never-grow-up
Cowardice	Non-nurturing
Demanding	Patronizing
Egotistical	Talk big, deliver small
Emotionally constipated	Temperamental
Flatterer	Thinking with the little head
Hard-headed	Unfaithful
Hunger for attention	Ungrateful
Immature	Unrealistic
Insensitive	Unreliable
Irresponsible	Vain

MEN'S POSITIVE QUALITIES:

Adventurous
Aggressively voices opinions at work
Analytical
Bighearted
Bold
Carefree about style and image
Dominating
Focused on work, not their looks
Forgive and forget
Fulfills family obligations
Generous
In control
Logical
Loving (towards his wife and mistress)
Networking
Nonemotional
Not devious
Not a slave to fashion
Not petty-minded
Open-minded
Physically strong
Protector
Says what's on his mind
Scientific
Sharing knowledge

WOMEN'S NEGATIVE QUALITIES:

Being men's sex object
Bossy
Dare not take a risk
Emotional
Envious
Fear of loosing face
Fickle
Gossiping
Indecisive
Inferiority
Inferiority complex
Insecure
Jealous
Lack of confidence
Lack of mobility
Moody
Nagging
Narrow-minded
Not seeing the big picture
Not vocal enough
Perfectionist
Petty
Petty-mindedness
PMS
Possessive
Power-craving
Revengeful
Self-centered

WOMEN'S NEGATIVE QUALITIES (cont.):

Selfish
Sensitive
Submissive
Timid
Two-faced
Ungrateful
Vain
Weaker body

WOMEN'S POSITIVE QUALITIES:

Accommodative
Adaptable
Analytical
Approachable
Beautiful
Caring
Charming
Committed
Compassion
Cool
Creative
Dedicated
Detail-minded
Down to earth
Empathy

Endurance
Flexible
Focused
Forgiving
Graceful
Hard-working
Honest
Independent
Intuition
Loyal
Meticulous
Neat
Organized
Passionate
Patience
Practical
Resilience
Resourceful
Responsible
Self-disciplined
Sensitivity
Sincere
Smart
Survivors
Thinking before talking
Thinking with their big head
Understanding
Visionary
Voluptuous
Willing to learn
Wisdom

WOMEN'S WEAKNESSES THAT MANIFEST IN THE WORKPLACE:

Always wanting to please
Can't deal with office politics well
Complacency
Dare not take a risk
Don't share knowledge
Don't stand up to men
Emotional
Family comes first
Fear of losing face
Grant favors unfairly
Indecisive
Inferiority
Insecure
Instigating
Jealousy
Lack of confidence
Lack of mobility
Low self-esteem
Narrow-minded
No killer instinct
Non-confrontational
Not seeing the big picture
Not adventurous

Not ambitious
Perfectionist
Petty
Possessive
Power-craving
Self-centered
Selfish
Shyness
Take things personally
Too empathetic
Too submissive
Too kindhearted
Two-faced
Ungrateful

Balancing Masculine And Feminine Qualities

After looking at the positive and negative qualities ascribed to both genders, I see some contradictions and false assumptions. The list is not about men and women, rather it is about the expression of feminine and masculine qualities. Certain women possess a great deal of masculine qualities while some men are dominated by feminine qualities.

We think of emotions such as love, insecurity, self-limitation, self-doubt, worry, fear, jealousy, envy, and shame as feminine, but in fact they are shared equally by both men and women. Females have no exclusive rights to being "overly" emotional.

During one of my seminars, Georgette asked me how she could have more time; she found that she was constantly overworked. As I kept asking her questions, digging deeper, I discovered that she did not have a time problem. Instead, what she perceived of as her lack of time was actually a fear of offending—to the extent that everyone unloaded their work in her direction.

At the afternoon session, Georgette had another question about one of her subordinates from Holland who was hard to control. This subordinate acted as if she were the department head instead Georgette. After I worked with her a little more, she realized that both her lack of time and her problem with her subordinate were both rooted in her wimpy personality.

This story reads perfectly because Georgette is a female. In fact, Georgette is a fictitious name; the star of the story is actually a man. You see, being wimpy is not the sole provenance of women; men possess this quality in equal measure.

Go back through the men and women's positive and negative qualities and check which ones apply to you. If you find you are short on your masculine qualities, then you may have to work at incorporating them by hanging around some masculine men. Select their admirable qualities and try to integrate them into your personality.

Water finds its course
according to the shape of the ground.
The warrior achieves victory by devising strategies
according to the conditions of the enemy she is facing.
So, as water has no fixed form,
warfare has no fixed rules.
—Sun Tzu (6.30)

A man will marry a totally cute, feminine girl—even a *really* dumb girl, but he will never, ever make her the CEO of his company. In order to rise in your chosen field, it is good to possess equal parts of feminine and masculine. Before you can master the 'real thing," your wardrobe can help to some degree to achieve that more balanced appearance. If you are too masculine, try to choose some feminine colors or a softer fabric blouse under your masculine business uniform. If you are too feminine, put on the dark banker's suit for change. Of course, if you are a well-balanced perfect woman, then, no matter what you wear, you will always represent the portrait of the perfect woman.

In the workplace, being capable alone is not enough. Even capable women are a dime a dozen, but the one who means business and *shows* her leadership through a balance of her masculine and feminine power is that rare diamond among a mountain-full of crystal rocks.

141

I am in a woman's body,
with a lion's heart.

> *—Queen Elizabeth I*

BECOMING POWERFUL

*One must be able
to move as swiftly as the wind,
to stand as still as the forest,
to be as destructive as
the fire sweeping the prairie,
to be impenetrable as the thick clouds,
to be as active as the thunderbolts.
—Sun Tzu (7.16)*

While speaking at a conference attended by high-powered businessmen—charter members of the rich and powerful, I chanced to audit a workshop for their trophy wives. I must say I have never encountered a sadder, more despairing group of women. One after another, they shared their stories of how the only one who mattered in their family was the husband; and his business, his needs always come first. None of these women felt any personal dignity. The tears in the room flowed not in drops, but in buckets.

The husband's role is to provide and protect, but in reality some provide and abuse. The meaning of the trophy wife's whole existence is to cater to every need and pleasure of her trophy husband. While these women's tears are directed towards their husbands, underneath they are the source of their own pain due to their lack of internal power.

For women, claiming power can feel very unfamiliar. We've been trained to look to others to give us our power, to seek permission to be powerful. It's time to change that. In reality, no one will *give* you power. You have to claim what is yours. And only when you are in touch with your own abundance of power, can you empower others (your employees, your children, your friends, etc.)

For men and women alike, the lack of personal power is the root of all of our problems. You may feel offended by my statement, however, there is no nicer way to put it—it is just a fact of life. If your best friend borrows money from you, but hesitates to pay you back, the problem is not within your friend—it is due to your own lack of power.

Your friend will pay those bills that she must pay, according to whom she cannot get away from without paying. If you fight with your lover or husband a great deal because you think he does not respect you, he is not the problem—you are. Your lover can intuitively sense your powerlessness and your lack of self-respect, so he treats you accordingly.

If at your office people are taking unfair advantage of you, look no further—you are the cause of the other's behavior. The world abuses those that it perceives are weak and wimpy; be they men or women, young or old, at work or on the playground.

It is impossible to try to describe what power feels like to anyone who is a stranger to power. To those who know about power, they know each person has a unique experience of their own particular ordeal. The key elements of the power inherent in each woman have little to do with being confrontational; the deepest secret is that it is all about capturing and exhibiting the proper attitude: "I am the source of power. I am powerful."

Power, according to the dictionary, means: "the ability to do or act; capability of doing or effecting something; strength; might; the possession of control or command over others; one who or that which possesses or exercises authority or influence." But none of these explanations really capture the essence of power.

When I speak of power without giving it a definition, we all understand that the power I speak of is within each one of us. It is an actual, tangible force that manifests through our feeling and experience. Without possessing power within first, how can we exercise it to accomplish our desires or influence others? This clear, unmistakable experience of power must reside and originate within us. If the power is within us, the question remains, "How can you and I manifest this power?"

Here are the six steps to being powerful:

1. Find out Where the Power Is Not

When we can eliminate all of the wrong places to look for power, then, what is left is the source of pure power. Power does not come from your job title or your bank account or your position or your family name. Power is embedded in you; it's up to you to find it. I will make this point more clearly by sharing with you a true-life story.

Dr. Narita was born in Japan under a lucky star. Her father was politically well-positioned (he had served as a cabinet minister to his government), he possessed great financial acumen and was influential in the upper echelons of Japanese society.

Dr. Narita was an obedient daughter; she had studied hard and graduated from a prestigious medical school. Twenty five years ago she came to the United States to serve her internship. Being a superior student and a hard-working intern, she was offered a position at a prestigious clinic being formed by a group of the medical school's professors. Years later, she became a full partner in the clinic. Everything was going her way until six years ago.

Trouble began to brew when her eighty-five year old father's health started to fail. Dr. Narita spoke to her father about her desire to inherit his television and radio conglomerate in Japan. At first, her father was against the idea because he thought his daughter too green in the real-world ways of power struggles and money management, but he could not withstand her begging. The old gentleman gave in and persuaded the other stock holders to give his daughter a chance to run this business which he had built from the ground up.

Out of respect for the wishes of their founder, the board agreed to let Dr. Narita take over the business. Dr. Narita was deliriously happy. By now, she was fifty years old and tired of her routine clinical work. She sold her interest in the clinic, packed up her family, and returned to Japan.

Three years, after Mr. Narita had passed away, Dr. Narita, at the age of fifty-three, for the first time found herself unemployed. She had been thrown out by a majority vote of the board due to what they assessed as poor leadership. With no alternatives left, she took a position at a Japanese hospital. I saw her shortly after she assumed her leadership position in her father's business. She was wearing a six caret ruby ring and had her own chauffeur to transport her around town in the company-owned Mercedes sedan. I saw her again recently, sans the jewelry and arriving by Tokyo subway. During our last meeting she confided to me through tears of deep despair, "Now I have no power."

I looked at her and thought to myself that here was a lady who does not have the faintest clue as to what power is about. She was handed a position with power, yet, since she was powerless inside, she could not sustain and thrive in her inherited position. She knows every power broker in the country; all of whom, at one time or another, had benefited from their relationship with her father. Even though these people wanted to repay their debt to her father who had helped them, they could not be of help to her because they recognized that she was powerless in spirit.

Dr. Narita is right, she has no power. But she thinks that she has no power now because her present work is in a position which does not come with power. What she does not know is that power comes from within first; then the proper position is granted to decorate that power outside. For her, power came from the outside first and, because of an attendant lack of power within, she could not hold on to the power position outside.

Whatever power you possess from within will surely manifest outside. Conversely, when you are empty of power within, even if you are given a kingdom it will be taken away from you.

2. You Don't Need Permission to Take Your Power

Many women are fighting to get permission to be in positions of power. Power is not something you wait for someone else to hand to you or that you wait until you get permission to exercise it. *Power is that which you take control of; you seize.*

Once, I gave a keynote speech to over one thousand top salespersons who work for the IBM Corporation in the Asia-Pacific region. Asia is the most profitable export market for IBM. Each of the attendees had made sales worth many millions of dollars for their company. During the ceremony, they acknowledged seven premiere producers. As their names were being called, the first five were women and three of them were very pregnant.

All the women participating applauded; everyone, including all of the male participants, loved the idea that strong women were winning. The illustrative fact is that women *are* powerful and we can manifest our power, regardless of the culture we live in or our nationality. The only requisite is that we be willing to be self-assured, and exhibit our innate, inner power.

3. Discover Where the Power Is

Power begins with an experience or awareness that we feel within us, but where is it located? In my big toe or on top of my head? Is power tangible or intangible? Power is commonly understood as intangible; but, to the person who possesses power, it is tangible and real. I would like to give you an experience of power's manifestation within you that will put you in direct touch with your power. When you contact your inner power, you will then be able to consciously direct, manifest, and manipulate it in the outside world.

Close your eyes. Focus your attention and mental feeling inside your body in your heart region. Mentally push your awareness and go deeper and deeper into your heart; become quieter and quieter. When your restlessness subsides, feel the sensation of that peace which lies there as a ground base in your being.

Follow your breath, let your mind sink lower and lower into the center of your being. Breathe deeply into your abdomen. Let your mind immerse itself into your breath. Let go of your intellectualization and disappear both the concepts of the mind and the heart; evaporate the conflict of the heart and the mind. In return, feel you are in touch with a new dimension of energy. This energy is pulsating with aliveness and certainty; it also has its own sense of direction—this is the sensation of power.

Although this power is always inside all of us, for most of us who are not used to utilizing and manifesting our power to any great extent, we cannot find our power when we need to use it. Because we are creatures of habit, even the locating and the utilization of power is also born out of habit.

4. Imitate Nature

That power which is within us also takes form in the universe as the power of nature. Sun Tzu speaks of a powerful army looking like the working of the wind, forest, fire, mountain, clouds and thunderbolts. By understanding what a powerful army looks like, we can come to understand what a powerful woman looks like.

Wind, Forest, Fire, Mountain, Clouds, and Thunderbolts are the manifestations of power in nature. For you to get a dosage of instant power, picture these forces and contemplate on their essence.

• *The wind or hurricane sweeps everything in its way.* It blows without hesitation. The wind is detached from the effect that it has on the earth; be it positive or negative. It is only true to its own agenda and objective.

• *The forest consists of many trees that have stood for hundreds of years.* These trees have seen humans born and die, battles fought and lost, corpses lying on the ground and returning to dust. While the human drama unfolds ceaselessly the forest remains unmoved; absorbed in its own joy of existence.

• *The fire burns with total freedom without consideration for the consequence of the objects on its way.* Fire doesn't seek permission to burn the woods. She burns with a single focus and is totally absorbed in her own objective.

• *The mountain is steady and immovable.* When facing changes, the steady and unchanging mountain silently observes the chaos of motion around it.

• *The clouds are thick enough to cover over the brightest of the sun's rays.* Within the thickness of the clouds, all things mysterious conceal themselves.

• *The thunderbolt strikes ruthlessly and without mercy.* The thunderbolt can be a source of electrical power or the demon of destruction, yet the thunderbolt makes no judgement of its merits. It is detached from your judgement. The thunderbolt is just being true to its own nature.

These six forces, are fierce, specific and detached. Contemplate their qualities and try to see how we can imitate their power to help us accomplish our noble tasks.

5. Practice "I Am"

• *Create a mental image and then focus on that image. Declare to yourself, "I am."* You have to operate your life from the position that you already are, not that you are trying to be.

Not long ago, I consulted for a Asian presidential candidate. He entered into the presidential race close on the heels of having lost a recent campaign for governor. Because of the memory of his ignoble defeat, I noticed that he was trying harder than ever in his new campaign for the presidency.

Clearly on television everyone could see that he was trying to be the next President. No one votes for someone who is trying—people vote for she or he who looks and acts like the President.

I told him, before he delivered each speech, he must repeat the mantra, "I am the President," until it became a reality for him. I further advised him to live his life by every instant expressing the conviction in his heart that he had already attained the office of President. From that moment on, everyone could see an incredible difference in his personal manner. He had become presidential. In three weeks, he jumped from third position in the race to leading in the polls. The end result was that he became the President of a Pacific-Asian country.

• *Holding onto the sensation of "I am", become aware of your physical sensations.* Do you feel taller and sit or stand straighter? Do you raise your head a little higher? What kind of changes have occurred in your facial expression? Do you feel calmer and more relaxed?

• *After getting in touch with the power of "I am," deliver your communication in any suitable manner of voice—it can be stern or soft.* It is not the tone of voice that matters; it is not even the words you choose to say that matters; it is the spirit in which you deliver your communication.

a. This spirit that you put behind your voice is directional, filled with certainty and the power of "I am." When you want to sell a product or service to a potential buyer, you can't just think "I am going to try to sell him something." You need to experience from the depth of your soul that you have sold him your product already. Therefore, when you speak to him, your voice will be filled with directive power. You will then see how easy he will come along.

b. While you are speaking, joking around with your counterparts, coworkers, staff or bosses, never for a moment lose your sense of "I am."

c. "I am. Thus, I am." That which we declare ourselves to be, we become—it is a mathematical certainty, for it works on so many levels that we are not even aware of. This also works for both negative as well as positive self-programming. So, be careful of what states you let your mind dwell in.

6. Be Detached and Focused

When we're too attached to consequences—the commission, the job, or even someone's feelings—we undermine our own clarity and we actually lose our power. The actress auditioning for a role needs to focus on her part, not on whether she gets the job. The saleswoman needs to focus on providing the best service to her customer, not on her commission. The friend that is too concerned about your feelings to speak openly and honestly to you does you a disservice *and* gives away her power. It is important to detach from the outcome and stay focused on the wellness of your customer/child/friend.

Once, during a seminar, a very sweet girl asked me, "How can I collect my money from a friend without jeopardizing our friendship?" It seems many kind-hearted people have this common experience about the difficulty in collecting borrowed money from friends. What is so amazing is that her friend took her money and refused to pay her back as agreed, yet, she was attached to their friendship. The same thing goes for your lover, when you cannot live without him, he senses your powerlessness. When you don't have to have him in your life, then he will sense your power—and power is the greatest aphrodisiac.

When I feel most powerful is when my spirit is detached from all the fruits of my actions and the desires of the world while my mind is laser-sharp and focused in a definite direction with a clear purpose and objective. When you cannot live without the objective of your desire, you became powerless and emotionally naked. When you are willing to not have the objective of your desire, you find that within that detachment, there is the seat and heart of your power.

When you realize that
you are trapped and surrounded,
you will become fearless.
When you have no way out,
you will tap into your courage
to stand firm.
When you have no choice,
you will fight back
with all your might.

—*Sun Tzu (11.33)*

The first thing you did after you were born was open your big mouth and cry. You were born natural, free, complete, and without pretension. You were a powerful, natural warrior. You were born with more than enough power necessary to break through your life's obstacles.

Somewhere, you lost that natural womanhood. With the awareness of your personal power, you can return to what you truly are—a naturally powerful human. This is *di*, the landscape our Maker has provided. Use it well. By regaining what you already are, you become mighty in your own potentiality.

BECOMING POWERFUL

Chin-Ning Chu

IV. JIANG—LEADERSHIP

*A leader must be wise, trustworthy,
benevolent, courageous, and strict.*
            —Sun Tzu (1.6)

*If you have never been hated by your child,
you have never been a parent.*
— *Bette Davis*

GOOD MOTHER, GOOD LEADER

Hence the saying: The intelligent leader
lays her plans well ahead.
The good general fine tunes
her operation carefully.
—Sun Tzu (12.16)

Napoleon said, "Leadership is everything." The leader is the one who wins the battles by designing the grand strategies of winning, and then commanding and motivating her troops to execute her plans. Leadership is not about your job title; it is all about your attitude. We women seldom see ourselves as leaders; mothers especially (we see ourselves more like maids!). And yet leadership is not unfamiliar to women; every woman has at some time assumed the role.

On the playground you may have led your sisters or brothers, at home you lead your children, at church you take a leadership role on Sunday picnics. We don't think of this as leadership, we think of it as the stuff of everyday life. If we are to turn the 21st century into the Woman's Century, we have to stop waiting for somebody to lead us or to give us the position so we can lead. We must embrace the attitude of leadership.

A Good Leader Leads By Leading

I spoke of this story in my last book, *Do Less, Achieve More*. After a speaking engagement in Lima, Peru, I decided to visit Machupichu, a site of ancient Incan pyramids. Peru is a difficult place for foreigners to get around in, so I had paid for a deluxe travel package that guaranteed me the best of accommodations.

After I got off the train in Machupichu, my local tour guide was supposed to meet me at the station's platform. He was nowhere to be found. I followed the swarming crowd towards the exit door. The exit door led to a zig-zag Disneyland-type waiting line with aluminum handrails. At the end of the rail was a group of buses.

Very official-looking people were directing everyone to get onto the buses. In the meantime, I tried to ask how to get to Machupichu. The answer was, "Get on the bus."

After a ride on a narrow and winding dirt road to the top of the mountain, I was flushed out of the bus to face the ancient pyramid city of the Incas. I quickly realized that this was not where I was supposed to be; I was to have been brought to my hotel first. It turns out my beautiful hotel was actually at the bottom of the hill, just a short distance from the train station. Now it dawned on me why the other bus riders had no luggage—they were returning back to Cuzco that afternoon. There was no way I could visit the pyramids with all of my luggage.

I had to get down the hill. I paid some local people to telephone my hotel and ask them to send a car to get me. At first I was told a car was coming. Forty minutes and several phone calls later, I was told no car was coming, and I was supposed to take a bus down.

With fifteen buses parked there, not one would go to the bottom of the hill because there were just five of us who wanted to leave—me, my husband, an Australian man and a couple from South Africa.

After waiting another hour, it dawned on me that this was all wrong. I got up and walked through the sidewalk cafe, shouting, "Who wants to get back to town?" Forty people got up and moved towards the bus. The bus's capacity was only about thirty-five, so there were people left standing.

I saw it clearly: nothing gets done unless you have a leader. The fact that most people don't see themselves as leaders means more opportunities for you. When you're in a situation that requires leadership, take the reins. The way you lead is simply by leading.

Leadership Is A State Of Mind

Leadership is in the spirit of the individual not in the job title. Leadership is not about force but about strength and direction; it is not a behavior, it is a focus. We can be gentle leaders at home and firm-handed leaders at work; these are not in conflict.

Leaders are not only found in business or military camps; they also exist in the family. One who has empathy and understanding and who can earn trust and provide direction is a good leader, whether at home or at work. When we can't control our children, when we are doormats at home, when our kids step on and abuse us, there is no way that we can be effective leaders at work, even if we have an engraved nameplate with the title "Leader" on our desk.

It is ludicrous to think that one can be a mouse at home and, just by taking a ride to the office, suddenly transform into a tiger. If your work calls for the power of a roaring tiger, be a roaring tiger; and if at home what's needed is a gentle pussycat, be that gentle pussycat. Both the tiger and the pussycat can be effective leaders; it's all a matter of the state of your mind.

Good mothers and good leaders share five important qualities:

1. Wisdom

A leader at work must be wise in her vision and knowledgeable in her technical competency to manifest her visions. In another words, she had better be good at what she does in order to bring forth the profit and satisfaction for her workers and her company.

By the same token, a mother must also be wise to provide guidance for her children as well as help support her husband during his trying times. She needs to carry out all the daily tasks of managing a household and looking after her family's needs. She also needs to plan for her children's futures, and then put that plan into action. Wisdom, direction, vision, guidance, and proficiency are the manifestation of a wise mother and a wise leader.

2. Trustworthiness

We come into this world with total trust and then, as we get battered around by life, we learn distrust. By the time we get to our work lives, distrust is a way of life. Therefore, a leader at work must *earn* the trust of her people or they will come to doubt her ability to lead the company to a long and prosperous future. Her employees, while working for her, will be using all their work hours to contact head-hunters, seeking their next job, instead of focusing on doing their work.

If she is not trusted by her bosses, investors or stockholders, she will not be able to function freely to manifest her vision. Her superiors will interfere and attempt to micro-manage her. If she delivers an inferior product or after-sales support that leads to distrust by her customers, she will lose her credibility for herself as well as her company, thus resulting in a loss of revenues.

A leader must also ask herself: do I trust my employees, my partners, and my investors? Are they worthy of my trust? If the answer is "no," then you have a serious problem. Ask yourself: how can I turn this around? Can the various breakdowns of trust be addressed and resolved?

The same goes for a mother. Without the trust of her children, her wisdom and guidance will be no use to them. Her children will have excommunicated her, mentally. She will become clueless about what is going on with them. When teenagers get pregnant and secretly have abortions or take drugs, it is because they don't trust their parents enough to pour out their pain to them. When there is no trust, there is no communication; then there is no understanding.

Without the benefit of their mother's experience, our children are in a dark confusion trying to sort out this complex world. All because there is no trust. Just as the business leader must earn the trust of her staff, her customers, etc., the mother must not take for granted that her children must trust her; she must take her time to understand where trust has been shattered and work hard to restore it.

3. Benevolence

Benevolence is not being a doormat; it is a radiating outward of personal power and an ability to include differing opinions. It is a quality that comes from strength and inner security. A benevolent leader will gain the love and support of her fellow workers and partners. A benevolent leader is not threatened by being told what she has done wrong; instead she feels indebted to a staff that is honest and direct in this way. A benevolent leader instills the sense of equality among her management team and workers; duties may vary, but opportunity and basic human dignity are equal. She makes people feel good about working for her.

It is the same for the benevolent mother. She accepts and understands her children's viewpoints. The mother who mercilessly imposes her values and rules upon her children becomes toxic and abusive. A mother's benevolence is not like the Gestapo chanting the slogan, "This is for your own good." Rather, the benevolent mother tries to understand even the behavior that she finds hard to comprehend. Only through benevolence can you hope that your children will come to trust you and be open to your wise guidance.

4. Courage

A proficient leader is a forward-thinking woman. If not, in time, her work will become outdated and obsolete. However, it takes courage to be forward-thinking and forward-acting. Forward-thinking and acting means change. When you make changes, you face risks and uncertainty. In business, if you are bold enough to made drastic changes, you face the possibility of a chaos that can translate into a drop in short-term revenue.

To make it through the change to a new way of doing business and the possibility of greater growth in the future, you will have to give an extra effort to sustain your existing business revenue. These kinds of moves take guts. If you experience a temporary set back, you have to face your board of directors, investors and your bosses's finger-pointing.

Leaders cannot lead without courage, however, don't attempt anything drastic unless you are very technically competent in your field and you can give affirmative answers to the following questions:

Do I possess the ability to be decisive?
Do I have the guts to push forward the necessary tasks?
Am I willing to take the calculated risks?

Do I have the stomach to handle the unpredictable temporary setbacks?
Do I possess an uncrushable strength?
Do I have the ability to bear humiliation?
Can I endure trying times?

Whether it may be used in attaining personal goals or your company objectives, mental toughness is vital to the success of a working woman. If one cannot handle the pain of setbacks, one should not enter the battlefield of life and business in a leadership role.

Joanne, an entrepreneur and the CEO of a sizeable company, was a defendant in a lawsuit that lasted for eight years which had been imposed by the state of California due to a business decision she had made. At the end of the eight year ordeal, she won the lawsuit, however, she had gone though eight years of hell. The incident did not destroy her; it made her tougher than ever and, in the meantime, her business grew and prospered.

During my seminar, she told me, "I was very moved when you were reading the words, 'Even the greatest warrior, when standing in the midst of the battlefield, sweats with fear. However, while her body is fearful and her mind is fearful, her spirit is fearless. She is able to detach herself from the fear of the body and the mind, clinging instead to the fearlessness of her spirit.' That is exactly what I went through." A courageous leader is not without fear, rather, in spite of her fear, she faces her challenges and does what must be done.

It is no different for a mother. It takes great courage for a mother to trust her kids. It takes great courage to face the consequences of a kid's minor and major mischief. The reason kids don't tell their parents about their misdeeds is that they know that if they do tell, they will encounter their mother's fear—fear of additional trouble to her already challenged life. And that fear easily triggers blame, anger, and rage. In spite of the love a mother might have for her kids, without the courage to face what trouble kids can stir up in life, a mother is often inept at being truly benevolent. It is courage that gives birth to trust, benevolence, and wisdom. Courage allows you to earn the grace of your kids.

5. Strictness

On the battlefield, a good commander sets strict standards for performance regarding rewards and reproach. If the standard is clear and strictly enforced, then people will perform their duties; otherwise discontentment will arise. A strict leader will not reward, due to her personal preference, those who are unworthy. Strictness is not something that applies only to your staff, it also applies to your relationship with your bosses, partners and even to your customers.

A friend of mine owned a small custom software house. By not setting strict performance expectations with their clients, they allowed several key customers to flip-flop again and again on a software design, a situation that served no one in the end. Eventually they ended up with upset customers and a disastrous situation that caused them to go out of business. If they had held their customer's feet to the fire and insisted that they stick to what they had agreed upon or had them pay extra for the alterations, they could have avoided failure.

This applies just as well to a good mother. While she is strict with her children, she is even stricter with herself. You can't expect your children to be disciplined and act from a high moral standard if you aren't disciplined yourself. At first, strictness may seem in conflict with tolerance and benevolence; it is not. When you are too strict without compassion, you create a rebellious child. With too much benevolence, you can create a spoiled brat who ends up spinning out of control. Good mothering, like good business leadership, lies in the balancing of paradoxical forces: benevolence with strictness, wisdom with ignorance, courage with fear, effort with ease.

ॐ

When there is frequent commotion in the camp,
it indicates the absence of strong authority.
When the banners and flags are seen shifting about,
it indicates rebellious activities.
When the officers easily get angry,
it indicates that they are tired.
                              —Sun Tzu (9.31)

The superior leader is the one who can engulf a multiple spectrum of realities. From the subtle matters of discipline and the understanding of her people, to the gross reality of technical savvy and integration of all these aspects into a seamless whole.

This is what a good leader does in her office: she plans the strategies, translates them into tasks, delegates the work, supervises the execution, and finally checks the results. She then seeks to detect problem areas that need improvement, and follows this by altering her strategies to provide for a more effective execution in the future.

This is also what a good mother does at home. By taking care of the financial planning for her children's college fund for example, she looks at the big picture of her family's future, and then puts this vision into executable steps. She may interview financial consultants or check websites for suitable investment programs. After analyzing the performance of her investments and making adjustments to her strategy, she then re-executes her plan. Eventually, when her son or daughter is ready for college, she has the money available for them.

A leader leads by leading. Even if you have never been in a leadership position at work, start to see yourself as an experienced leader. Start to volunteer your leadership in social and professional activities at work or after work to show off how you might shine as a leader. Lead with wisdom, cultivate trust, exercise benevolence, incorporate courage, and don't be afraid to be strict. This is the picture of *jiang* that Sun Tzu envisioned.

Those who are really in earnest
are willing to be anything or nothing
in the world's estimation, and publicly,
in season and out, avow their sympathies
with despised ideas and their advocates,
and bear the consequences.
—Susan B. Anthony

YOU CAN'T LEAD UNLESS YOU KNOW YOURSELF

Not knowing your opponent,
but knowing yourself;
the chance for victory is fifty-fifty.
Not knowing your opponent or yourself;
one hundred battles, one hundred defeats.
—Sun Tzu (3.23)

The degree to which you know the universe in which you live is in direct proportion to how well you know yourself. A good executive knows what is right for her people. A superior salesperson can read her customer's unspoken demands. An understanding mother can sense something is wrong with her daughter or son. A considerate wife can detect whether her husband had a good day at work. You can't always depend on others to tell you what they want from you because often they can't tell you the truth, or they don't know what the truth is, if they are not in touch with their feelings.

In Matthew 13:13, Jesus Christ spoke of how little we know ourselves: "...they seeing, see not; and hearing, they hear not; neither do they understand." Socrates, the greatest of the Ancient Greek philosophers, also taught as his central core concept, "Know thyself." Sun Tzu and all great teachers imparted this idea as the basic foundation for the human pursuit of excellence.

The injunction to "know yourself" is, needless to say, easier said than done. If it were so easy, everyone would do it and it would not be the key that holds the fate of a hundred victories.

In front of the Sun Tzu Museum in his hometown in China is a magnificent stone carving of just eight letters. It states: *"Know yourself, know others; one hundred battles, one hundred victories."* Knowing yourself and knowing your opponents sums up the essence of Sun Tzu's *Art of War*. It is not by accident that Sun Tzu placed "know yourself" before "know your opponents." The superior execution of everything we have learned thus far, and everything in the upcoming chapters, depends on how well you know yourself.

If you are clueless about yourself, then it will be hopeless for you to attempt to know what is going on around you. You cannot think of leading others, until you know how to lead yourself. You can not lead yourself until you know something about yourself.

The following concepts are put forward for your consideration of how exactly you are going to come to know *you*.

Steps that will lead you to know you:

1. You must Possess a Strong Desire to Know Yourself

Most persons do not see the need for self-examination until something terrible happens that causes them to be in deep mental agony. These costly lessons are meant to give you a wake-up call. After you have gone through the finger-pointing stage, if you are lucky, you will start to see that it is necessary for you to explore within yourself ; that you are holding the key that will unlock why things are not going right.

Maryann tried very hard to lose weight and get fit. She signed up at the spa, and exercised and ate well. After being on her program for three or four days, she started to feel better. As soon as she felt slightly better, she would stop exercising and reward herself by going out on the town to stuff her face. She kept on saying that she wanted to have a better life when, in fact, she actually had a comfort zone that was located in "uncomfortableness."

The energy of feeling good actually made her feel uncomfortable. By feeling bad, she felt good. Maryann must really and truly want to feel healthy and fit, not just give it lip service. As long as feeling bad is really a familiar comfort zone for her, she will remain clueless as to why she never achieves her goals. Unless feeling bad begins to feel so bad she can't stand it, she will never have the strong desire to even discover the hidden game she is playing with herself.

2. Be Your Own Psychiatrist

For the privilege of knowing more about themselves, people pay billions of dollars to psychiatrists. For the woman who doesn't have the time or money to burn on a psychoanalyst's sofa, be your own policewoman. After all, what you are paying the psychiatrist to do is to get you to discover the mystery of you.

Not until Maryann started to be her own detective, did she notice there was a pattern. It was not Joe's fault for inviting her to dinner, it was not Abby's fault for asking her to a movie so she had to skip her dance class. It was her pattern of feeling good about feeling bad that was the main cause of her self-defeating attitude.

For anyone who is in sales, notice that sometimes there are certain days that you are flying on the magic carpet, and everything you touch turns into gold. While other days, you can't say or do anything right. Analyze what caused you to fly high or what made you drop low. Since most of us are clueless about why we do anything we do or feel, we cannot recreate our good days.

If you are a salesperson, being your own detective means that you notice, by being anxious in closing a deal, it causes you to push too hard during your presentation. Next time, when you are making another presentation, tell yourself that you don't need to make that sale, that you are just here to make it clear to your potential client whether your product is right for her or not. Hold back your anxiousness. If you find you have held back too much, to a point of becoming unexciting, try to be more assertive next time. In time, you will find that perfect place to rest your mind during your sales calls.

Being your own psychiatrist means noticing that certain people or a certain tone of voice causes you to shrink. Next time that happens, notice how that feeling of intimidation effects you. Whenever that feeling repeats itself, catch yourself before you automatically react by saying or doing things that will cause you to feel really stupid later.

Instead, you should flip up a stop sign in your mind. Take a deep breath, stretch your neck, expand your chest, pick yourself up, make yourself physically and mentally taller. Then decide if you should say something back to your offender or just be silent and notice the power within your open body posture and the calmness of your breath.

If you constantly do things that betray your own interest, then you need to find out why you go with the negative flow. Who were you trying to please? What are the possible psychological root causes or past incidents that might be associated with this repeated behavior? If you were told as a child to be nice to everyone, you may find yourself betraying your own interests by going along with others.

While your body is engaging in action, your mind needs to be a detective constantly on surveillance. When you watch yourself long enough, your deep hidden nature will reveal itself. You can do this more effectively by writing your insights down using pen and paper to scratch notes or even make drawings that describe your experiences. Separate the information from your mind; get it on to paper so you can see how your thoughts lead you to your behavior.

3. Install Some Stop Signs Between Your Mouth and Your Mind

Between the mind and the mouth you may have an "expressway" with no stop sign; install some stop signs. As you are making statements, do a continuous editing of your own thoughts. Sometimes, the habit of automatically responding dies slowly, but through repeating your corrections, it will die in time.

4. See Yourself Through Someone Else's Eyes

Often, everyone else can see us better than we can. Find someone who knows you very well and truly has your interest in mind. Ask them how they see you. Beware, when you are seeking others to be your mirror, if the mirror is distorted then the reflection is undependable.

Denise was a Fortune 100 company CEO. When she divorced her first CEO husband Roger, she said it was because after she had worked all day she didn't want to come home to another CEO and discuss business all night. Then, after divorcing her second husband John the poet she explained that John wanted her to be home every night and cultivate their relationship while she had to often work late at the office.

So Denise did not like being married to another executive, nor did she like being married to a househusband, either. Denise may know how to make millions for her company and herself, but she is clueless when it comes to her life companions. After two divorces,

Denise may begin to know that she knows nothing about what exactly she wants from a husband or if she needs a husband at all. When her friend Jan told her of her behavior, Denise cried out, "I can't believe it! Such an obvious thing I just couldn't see it. Is my mind so good at keeping me in the dark, or am I just too dumb to see myself?" It's good to have a supportive friend to act as a mirror and reflect yourself for you.

5. Dive into Yourself

There is a place deep, deep inside of you, where, if you dive deep into yourself, you can see yourself clearly. There is a primal state of self-knowledge that exists within each of us. This state of natural knowing can be a highly effective business tool when applied in your daily life.

When you attempt to understand yourself solely by judging your outward actions; it does not always reveal the whole story. When you can incorporate inner vision along with the outer detective work, the result is much more satisfactory.

One time while on vacation in Florida, out of nowhere, I became furious at my husband for shaking red pepper over the pizza. My rage was so high that I walked out of the restaurant. All the time I knew it was not about the food because I was not even hungry. I needed to find out what was really bothering me, so I lay down on a bench in the garden grounds and looked into the starry winter sky, pondering. An hour later the answer came.

I had been preparing a business project that all of the people around me had told me I should be doing and I, also, had all of the evidence that I should be participating in it. My mind tried to reason with me that I should be following this avenue. Laying on that bench looking into the night sky, suddenly out of nowhere—with no connection to any reality—I saw my upset was caused by the fact that deep inside of me I knew I should not start this project. It was the wrong thing to do. All of the sense of urgency from those around me, and my attempt to see what I wished to see—not what really was—caused me to not see that the project was not doable. When I opened up to my inner guidance, all of my fury vanished. I had nothing left but peace and certainty.

Try to look at your actions through the agency of your inner vision. The inner vision not only provides you with insight to yourself, it also provides you with the wisdom to know things that you didn't know that you knew. I have devoted chapters dealing with this in my other books on the technique of meditation. Meditation is the fastest way to dive into your center where peace, self-knowledge, and intuition dwell.

6. Through Trial and Error

Recently I was watching cable television; mindlessly switching the channels. I happened upon a Spanish film starring a fat lady that looked like a low-rent version of Sharon Stone. I switched channels, going on to other programs. An hour later, I was back to flipping channels again. By now, the Spanish film was over and the credits were rolling. There it was—Sharon Stone's name on the screen. I couldn't believe it. I went out to the video rental store and rented the film, *Sand and Blood.*

This film was made during the transition period that Sharon went through from being a cheap Sharon Stone look-alike to being the all-together, real Sharon Stone that we came to know in the film, *Basic Instinct.* For decades, Sharon was struggling to discover who she really was. When she finally discovered herself, the world discovered her.

Knowing yourself is a lifetime commitment, yet, it is vitally important. The degree to which you know the world you live in is in direct proportion to how well you know yourself. Trial and error are essential ingredients in the process of knowing yourself. However, unless you can discover the cause of your errors and then make the proper adjustments, trial and error has no merit in itself.

It is said,
when you have the total knowledge
of yourself and your opponent,
victory can be secured.
When you have a thorough knowledge
of heaven's timing
and the layout of the earth,
then your victory will be complete.
　　　　　　　　　　—Sun Tzu (10.26)

While you are on the treadmill of discovering and improving yourself, to others, you seem no different than the rest of them. Only you know you are not just like them, bumbling and bungling around unconsciously. You are on the path of unceasing self-discovery and self-improvement, exercising and perfecting your power so that you might fit to be an exceptional *jiang*—a leader.

We still live in a world in which
a significant fraction of people,
including women,
believe that a woman belongs
and wants to belong exclusively in the home.
—Rosalyn Sussman
(Nobel Prize-winning
medical physicist)

READING ANYONE'S CHARACTER

A commander's state of mind
can be altered
by the manipulation of his enemies.
—Sun Tzu (7-24)

People are getting cleaver, not so much by gaining in wisdom, but rather in learning how to hide their true character. Because of this, it is harder and harder to read people's true character and nature. Yet, it is essential for a good leader to have the ability to read people. One may be kind and genial at work, and a wife or husband abuser at home. One may be brave and aggressive, and directionless during a crisis. Others are outwardly sweet and seemingly considerate, and yet treacherous and cunning. One may express competency while being unable to deliver the results.

I have collected a number of art of war treatises that provide the best insights for understanding the character of your bosses/customers/competitors and employees:

How To Read Anyone's Character:

• *Debate with her/him to expose their true nature and philosophy on life.*

Once an Australian reader asked me to visit him in Australia in order to audit his training course. He proposed his intention of participating in a joint venture with me. Although I wasn't sure about the business opportunity he had proposed, I thought it won't hurt to explore it and, most of all, it would be lovely to spend a cold American winter month in the Australian summer sun. I bought two airline tickets and left with the idea that, if I didn't like his course, I would still have a great vacation with my husband.

During the first day of the course, I saw there were a lot of flaws with his teaching and his character. He let it be known that he considered himself to be greater than Christ, Buddha and Mahatma

Gandhi. Moreover, he had trained his children and handful of followers to respond with robot-like obedience (although they didn't see it that way). To me, his behavior resembled Adolf Hitler's with his followers using verbal violence as a controlling tactic.

I debated with him during his course. He started to avoid the issues I raised and became furious and very intolerant of anyone (me) who *dared* to question him. Right in front of me, his foxtail was exposed. Although he claimed that he had the solution for creating a prefect environment for humans, yet, when one had the audacity to debate with him, he showed himself to be nothing but a self-righteous, narrow-minded, egotistical hypocrite. I left the course the next day (it was scheduled for three weeks) and went on my great summer vacation with my husband in Australia.

• *Challenge her verbally to watch the changes of her inner state.*

Beware, gentle does it. If she is your boss or customer, you don't want to turn her to hating you because you have wounded her ego.

• *Discuss operational strategies with her in order to observe her knowledge about her job.*

If she is clueless about her job, in time, your department may be eliminated or cut back in size due to poor performance. You may want to know this ahead of time, in order to plan to move to a different department or different company.

• *Inform her as to the difficulties and challenges ahead, thus to know her courage.*

If she can not handle the pressure, it is better to know earlier rather than later.

• *Drink and party with her (if you drink), then observe what her real nature is after she has let down her guard.*

You will see some persons are very reserved, but after a few glasses of alcohol they can be very funny and humorous, while others may be vicious and violent after drinking.

• *Entrust her to handle money, then you will know her integrity.*

Jenny had an assistant who, during his first week, she wanted to fire him because she detected his tendency towards sticky fingers. After he repented so sincerely and told her it was all a big mistake, she forgave him. The problem was that she should have forgiven him and still fired him, anyhow. Instead, she let him work for her for another two and a half years while he did severe damage.

• *Assign work to her, then discover her competence.*

People are getting so cleaver—instead of performing work, many learn the art of lip service.

• *During the time of her misfortune, observe whom she befriends.*

When things are going wrong in one's life, we go back to what is most familiar and to the people we are most comfortable with.

• *During the time of her prosperity, observe who receives her charity.*

When she is rich, does she give to impress others in order to gain public praise or does she give out of the goodness of her heart?

• *During the time she holds high offices, observe whom she employs.*

Does she employ capable persons, or those with connections that can advance her personal interests?

• *During the time of difficulties, does she act unethically?*

• *During the time of poverty, can she be bribed?*

• *When she is tempted with sex, observe her steadiness.*

Some people, as soon as they get involved in a relationship, begin flowing in and out of the office absentmindedly.

Good Leaders Are Not:

• *Greedy.*
• *Jealous of other's competency and proficiency.*
• *Easily influenced by others gossip and opinions and taking delight in praise.*
• *Focused only on understanding others, yet knowing nothing about oneself.*
• *Indecisive.*
• *Enslaved by the pleasures of the senses.*
• *Malevolent and cowardly.*
• *Evasive and deceitful, paying only lip service, lacking in sincerity. (However, the lip service can be so convincing, you may be fooled just the same.)*
• *Lacking competence, yet possessing a great sense of self-importance.*
• *Given to taking action hastily.*
• *Filled with inertia and laziness.*
• *Lacking in courage.*
• *Competent, but lacking in the strength to carry out one's ideas.*
• *Cruel.*
• *Lacking in charisma.*
• *Lacking in the performance of charitable works for the needy.*
• *Unable to project future outcomes.*

- *Unable to prevent the leaking of top secret information.*
- *Unable to recommend deserving individuals for appropriate promotion.*
- *Unable to take full responsibility for her adversity.*

Great Leaders Possess The Ability To:

- *Recognize the situation of her opponents.*
- *Recognize by what methods she should proceed or constrict.*
- *Know the limitations of her resources.*
- *Recognize favorable timing for actions.*
- *Recognize the natural geographic elements and understand the advantages and disadvantages inherent in many given situation.*
- *Exhibit originality in strategic planning and provide her competitors with total surprise.*
- *Hold her plans in secrecy.*
- *Create harmony among her people.*
- *Generate common objectives among her people.*
- *Motivate others.*
- *Exhibit a compassionate attitude toward employees.*
- *Be open-minded toward everyone.*
- *Be diligent in the execution of her duties.*

Five Formulas To Motivate Your People:

- *Attract extraordinary talent by assuring them prestigious titles and generous salaries.*
- *Treat your people with respect and trust their ability to perform.*

- *Set clear standards of expectations for their performance, and praise or reprimand them accordingly.*
- *Inspire your people by setting performance standards.*
- *Notice all the "little right things" they have done, then praise them. Acknowledge their outstanding performance with bonuses or promotions.*

These treatises were written thousands years ago, yet they are as true now as they were then.

Both working for the wrong boss or working with an inferior staff can be damaging to one's career objectives. Recognizing this early can save you grave financial losses and reduce your emotional stress. Unless one has been hurt at least once, they may not appreciate how valuable these formulas are when they are put to work.

An adaptive leader, (*jiang*) will not only read this chapter, she will take these principles to heart and measure them against her bosses, staff and customers. The ability to read human character is the basic element of a masterful leader—a proficient *jiang*.

Chin-Ning Chu

V. FA—MANAGING

Organization and effectiveness in execution
signifies your proficiency
in managing people and affairs;
thus resulting in a maximizing
of all your available resources.
                    —Sun Tzu (1.7)

Never doubt that a small group
of thoughtful committed citizens can
change the world.
Indeed, it is the only thing that ever has.
                    —Margaret Mead

KEEP THE $ COMING IN

*One who is skilled in warfare...
will not depend on the food supplies that are
transported from the distant home country
for more than three days.
—Sun Tzu (2.6)*

Professional equality cannot be approached solely by demanding it from a gender perspective: "I am a woman, so I deserve to be treated equally." Nothing speaks louder than bringing in profit for the company. Whether one is a man or a woman, when anyone brings in the profit, he or she will be highly valued and treated like royalty. In this section, Sun Tzu provides a results-oriented, cost effective strategy on how to sustain your fighting troops in the battlefield with the minimum output for the maximum return. Whatever your position may be, you will find one of the following strategies will speak to you directly.

Keep the $ coming in for you and your company through:

• Practicing the "Eat What You Kill" Policy

The military equipment will be
supplied by the home country,
but the food for the troops will be
gathered from the enemy's warehouses.
When the troops' provisions
must be transported over a distance
it will cause the depletion
of the national treasure.
This will cause a hardship to the people.
    —Sun Tzu (2.7)

"Eat what you kill" is the secret to operating any corporate or entrepreneurial project. To translate this statement into today's modern marketing and sales terms: Create results.

Your employing company should provide you with all the necessary tools and training in order for you to win the battle and the war of market share. A saleswoman may draw a salary from the company, but they cannot be a burden to that company.

Like the lioness, you must quickly bring in the kills so that you can feed yourself as well as the rest of the company's employees. Otherwise, you and other nonproductive people will deplete the company's resources and cause hardship to the company owners and investors. If you remember this, you will always be valuable wherever you go, whatever you do. You will eat well throughout your life upon the open veldt of business—the corporate Serengetti.

• Reward Results

In order to motivate your troops
to capture the enemy's provisions,
you need to reward them with profit.
During the battle of the charioteers,
who ever first captures ten enemy charioteers,
should be honored and highly rewarded
to stimulate the morale.
                              —Sun Tzu (2.14)

As a manager, in order to motivate your sales people to bring in the financial results for your company, you should reward them generously. For those special individuals who make great contributions to the company's financial well-being, besides the monetary rewards and bonuses, the company should acknowledge them with promotions and honors.

Michelle was working for one of the international account-ing firms and was stationed in Paris. She was creative, aggressive, and hard-working—the kind of worker any company would be proud to have. She had put together several large international deals and had made her company twenty million dollars.

For her outstanding performance, she received a two thousand dollar bonus. She quit. Now, she is running her own company. Last year, she grossed a hundred million dollars. If you don't generously reward your superior performers, most likely, you will end up creating your own competition. In order to insure your own survival, generously reward those who bring in results for you.

• Close the Deals Fast

The most important element
of conducting warfare
is aiming for a swift victory and
avoiding a prolonged campaign.
—Sun Tzu (2.15)

All business objectives are focused towards getting that $ and closing the deal as soon as possible. Helen was very good at generating new business leads and networking with everyone from Tokyo to London. Then her boss, Terry, began to notice that whenever it came time for the contract to be finally closing, Helen would let the contract sit around on her desk for weeks—and sometimes even forget about them—while she got busy drumming up fresh, new leads.

Finally, Terry had to confront her with the fact that each time she went after new leads, it cost the company money for the international telephone calls and faxes; not to speak of the time and labor required. Yet, here she was; neglecting the contracts that were sitting right on top of her desk.

In Helen's business, it took six months to a year to take a lead from prospect to contract. Terry confronted Helen as to what her psychological block might be; why she wasn't closing the deals and rolling in the money. Helen finally realized that, instead of bringing in the victories by winning the battles, she was enjoying the feeling of conducting eternal warfare. Realizing this, she went on to become a top producer in her industry.

This principle also goes for the marriage proposal. If you have been dating Prince Charming for an eternity, and yet he is still not proposing, you need to expedite your closing as you would with any business transaction by first examining the reasons that have caused you not to close the deal.

There are numerous reasons for a guy to not want to propose: 1) He could be a confirmed bachelor or a gun-shy divorcee. 2) He could feel that if he gets the milk for free, why should he buy the cow? 3) He wants to get married, just not to you. If there is no hope to closing the deal, then leave him. Don't linger, unless you are using him as a free stud.

Whether it is business or relationship, it is important to close those deals that you can close and drop those deals that cannot close. While you are preoccupied with the deals that you have no hope of closing, you are blocking yourself from seeing other opportunities. Wheel the deal in, or wheel it out; either way, you can move on to the next item and keeping the $ flowing.

Chin-Ning Chu

• Sell Yourself First

She will win,
when her sovereign,
does not interfere with her campaign.
                    —*Sun Tzu (3.20)*

The only way you can insure that your sovereign (your boss) will give you a free hand to conduct effective warfare is that you have sold yourself successfully as a superior leader and administrator. If you have not sold yourself properly and gained his/her confidence, your boss cannot help but interfere.

No matter what your position is in life, you are always your first product—sell yourself first. Until you have sold yourself, there is no hope for you to sell any product, whether they be goods or services. In fact, it is much easier to sell you than to sell your products, because you usually have no direct control over the products that you are selling.

The product is often the brain child of a group of people you don't know, while you are the direct result of your own doing. Your parents gave you the essentials for being a human being, you have then contributed the rest by molding yourself to be the way you are today. As long as you are happy with what you have done, then selling *you* is a piece cake.

How you represent yourself will effect every aspect of your life—from getting a job and making a sale, to keeping a husband and gaining respect and love from your children.

If you haven't spent much effort on working to improve yourself physically or mentally by doing the right things and thinking the right thoughts, it will show. Then it will be hard to sell yourself—and even harder to sell your product. People do business with those that they like.

Make your self invaluable by bringing in the kill to feed yourself and others. How can anyone discriminate against you at your office, or anywhere else for that matter, when their survival is in jeopardy without you? This is the creative way of exercising the principle of *fa* by preserving yourself through your ability to keep the $ rolling in for you and your company.

Chin-Ning Chu

Far away there in the sunshine
are my highest aspirations.
I may not reach them,
but I can look up and see their beauty,
believe in them,
and try to follow where they lead.
                    —Louisa May Alcott

MANAGING YOUR STAFF AND YOUR CHILDREN

No commander should wage a war out of anger.
No general should fight a battle out of rage.
—Sun Tzu (12.18)

A manager should not spread her anger all over the office because of her lack of self control; a mother should not punish her kids because of her irritation. Most people think family and office work are in contradiction with each other—I do not agree. Rather, I see your family and work skills as complementary. Any mother who is successful in empowering and disciplining her children can easily transfer those skills to the office.

Your attitude and tone of voice may be different when speaking with your staff versus your kids, but the principles of nurturing, empowering, correcting and disciplining are the same. By the same token, if you learn to cultivate your staff's talent and help them to help themselves in realizing successful projects, you will transfer this experience to child rearing. Sun Tzu's points on managing a staff apply equally well to managing your family:

How to manage your staff and your family:

1. Don't Be Frustrated

Too frequent rewards to your troops indicate that you are at the end of your resources; too frequent punishment of your troops means that you are frustrated with your condition.

—Sun Tzu (9.38)

The reason you would reward your troops when they don't deserve it and punish them unjustly is because of your own frustration at your lack of direction and the necessary skill to guide your people in producing the wanted result. Instead of working overtime on your people, work on you to find out why you behave so desperately.

My friend Tina and her husband Ted owned a computer multimedia company. As the competition got tougher, many expected contracts vanished into thin air. In hopes of rolling in the next "big" deal, Ted needed his staff to stay on the job so that the office would look full when their potential clients came in for appointments. He wanted to give the impression the business was thriving, instead of dissolving.

Almost every day, on a casual or official basis, Ted would give motivational pep talks and treat his people to restaurants or take-out food treats. The more he talked, the more they ate, the faster his employees resigned. It was as if the employees could sense his desperation and decided to jump ship quick.

In the meantime, Tina would have ferocious arguments and finger-pointing sessions with their partner, Leo, who was in charge of the technical department. Finally, it all collapsed. As I looked at this situation, I reflected on how true Sun Tzu's words are.

Children behave just like our troops and staff. If we punish them too often, it indicates that they have won, and we have lost. We will have nothing but desperation and frustration. They will not listen, and are totally aware that we have no idea how to get them to be disciplined. If we praise them and reward them even though they don't deserve it, they will catch on quick, and they will have you over a barrel. You need to be more detached about your frustration with them, and not too desperate in seeking their approval.

2. Impose Discipline Appropriately

When you punish the soldiers (staff) too soon, before they grow attached to you, then they will not be loyal to you. Thus, they become useless to you. When the soldiers grow attached to you, and punishment is not enforced; they, too, will be useless to you.
—*Sun Tzu (9.45)*

Most managers never give a thought to the consequences her punishment will have on her people and office morale in general. It is amazing that when Sun Tzu wrote this book, he had never commanded any one at all, yet, he could see that the timing of punishing his soldiers was essential to the success of his warfare objectives.

The only way he could have understood these subtleties is that he had become very sensitive as to how the timing of punishment would effect a single person. Probably in Sun Tzu's case, he had first-hand experience with his son or other family members. By observing how one person reacts to a given situation, it will lead you to understanding that, under similar situations, most humans react alike.

This strategy is very relevant to step parents. It is always very difficult to be a step mother. You are not the child's biological parent, yet, you have taken on the responsibility of managing your step child by marrying the child's father. Your timing of discipline must be as considered as Sun Tzu's.

3. Love Them like Your Kids

When you take care of your troops as if they were your infant children, they will follow you wherever you may lead them. When you treat them as if they were your beloved sons, they will follow you unto death.
—Sun Tzu (10.20)

Sun Tzu is not interested in mothering a group of soldiers who are long on the courage to die, but short on the skill to win. In order to achieve his commander-in-chief's objective, Sun Tzu needs to create soldiers with the courage to die and the superior skills to stay alive; that combination leads to victory.

As a manager, when you take care of your people as if they are your children, you will gain their respect and loyalty. In order to achieve this, you must give them the training in business skills, as well as in the proper attitude of mind to accelerate far beyond their own expectations. The proper way to love your people is to make them winners.

It is easier for parents to buy love from their children by giving them money and things. But by so doing, when the kids are grown up, you will lose them. They will no longer need your money. It is much more difficult to be committed to loving them by cultivating an intimate understanding through communication.

To give love to your children is to be supportive in their academic studies as well as help them to understand the complexities of life which they are facing now and what will be their major challenges later in life. By loving them in this way, you will have their love and loyalty until death and beyond.

4. Don't Be Too Loving

When you are complacent with your troops (staff), your authority will be diminished. When you are too loving toward your soldiers (workers), you will cause them to disrespect your commands.
—Sun Tzu (10.21)

As Groucho Marks said, "I would not want to join any club that would have me as a member." This is the mystery of human nature—we despise those who are overly available to us. This rule is not just for our people, it also goes for our clients. When we are overly available to our clients, we lose our power to direct them and, therefore, to serve them. We are then guaranteed to lose them in the long run.

Tammy was a salesperson and her sales philosophy was to build a strong personal friendship with all of her clients through exchanging personal gossip. Terry, her boss, was reviewing her nighttime international phone bills. She discovered that Tammy often made eight or ten calls to the same client in the same night. Among them was a client in England which Tammy was having a hard time in collecting the money from; the client owed a mere fifteen hundred dollars.

Terry pointed out to Tammy that, by being so available to the client, she had lost the Englishman's respect totally. Terry reproached Tammy, "To him, your time is not valuable. You seem to have nothing going on besides him. You have been overindulging in your telephone calls with him for over six months. The deal was so simple, so routine.

"How could you have had that much to say to him; with some of the calls taking up to sixty minutes? Your phone bills are near fifteen hundred dollars. You lost his respect by gossiping with him so much and therefore, he knows you are weak and he doesn't have to pay you."

The principle for managing your troops, your staff, or your clients are the same as those for managing your children at home. Be caring, but not overindulgent; be concerned, yet never lose your authority, be compassionate, yet never compromise discipline.

Human beings are like predators in the jungle, subconsciously, we are always sizing up with, "Who is my prey and who should I respectfully obey?" Being overly easy-going is the quickest way to diminish your authority with your children as well as with your staff and your clients.

Karen believed love would conquer all. She indulged her child with no set boundaries. She let him take drugs, smoke, drink and abandon his schoolwork and eventually get expelled from high school.

She continued to give him love and reinforce how good he was. She spent a hundred-thousand dollars in rehabilitation with no result. The kid had no incentive to change. Whether he was good or bad, Karen would treat him the same in loving manner. When your children and your people are unmanageable, they are not the problem—you are.

5. Never Spoil Them

Over-indulgence will cause your people to degenerate into a group of disorderly, spoiled children that are useless to anyone.

—Sun Tzu (10.22)

Carl Von Clausewitz, the nineteenth century German author who wrote the most important Western book on the strategy of warfare titled *On War*, said, "An Army must lose that impulse to unbridled activity which is characteristic in human nature and submit itself to demands of a higher kind; to obedience, order, rule and method. An army which preserves its usual formations under the heaviest fire, never loses its sense of obedience, its respect and confidence in its leaders and training."

As a manager or a mother, you empower and discipline your staff and your children. There is a delicate balance between empowerment and discipline. Empowerment has a tendency to puff up a person's ego and enhance their sense of self-importance. Discipline often leads one's ego to feel temporally diminished. True discipline and empowerment is brought about through the proper training of keeping one's ego focused toward the desired objective.

6. Manage Your Staff the Same as You Manage Your Children

Managing a large group of people is exactly the same as managing a small group; it is all about the division of numbers.

—*Sun Tzu (5.1)*

Regarding the management of small and large groups of people, Sun Tzu had an unconventional insight that is worthy of our contemplating. I could not digest this statement for the longest time; then I started to compare the difference between the management structure of my fortune 500 clients and my own small staff. I suddenly realized that Sun Tzu had hit the nail right on; there is no difference in managing the small and the large—it is only question of magnitude.

Every detail, on the broad scale, must be considered just as carefully in a small environment as it must in the larger environment. Every aspect of marketing, systems engineering, accounting, manufacturing must be considered just as thoroughly in the small environment. The only difference is, in the large company you have two hundred people doing the accounting, and it should be broken down by departments and divisions.

In the small company you have one person doing the accounting, but that one person must use the same skill and attention to detail as the two hundred person department does in running their megacorporation. In fact, the people who manage ten thousand person companies are also, in reality, merely managing a handful of people.

From that top echelon, the commands are spread downwards to that handful of people at the first layers, and then multiplied. In China it is said, "Although the mocking bird is small, she possesses all of the same necessary internal organs as the largest of eagles."

If you have five kids that are driving you crazy, you may want to give yourself a break by adopting this theory of management. By effectively managing one, you can have he or she take the responsibility to help manage others.

My friend Belinda told me a great story that illustrated this point. She has three rottweilers. One is the mother and the two others are her babies. Belinda sent the two baby dogs to obedience school because they were acting like disobedient puppies. After spending fifteen-hundred dollars, the two little dogs had learned absolutely nothing.

Belinda then decided to change her strategy. Whenever the young dogs misbehaved, she would yell at the mother. She told the mother that she was such a bad dog for not managing her puppies.

Very soon the mother dog got the idea that it was her duty to teach her offspring to behave. Miraculously, in no time, the puppies became well-mannered young dogs fit for polite society.

Being a good manager is about effectively managing the key people, whether in the office, at home or even your dogs, then the desired positive results will appear.

7. Understand Your Group Dynamic

A proficient general directs one million soldiers as if she were holding one individual's hand; she can manipulate both with total freedom.
—Sun Tzu (11.38)

This strategy is very similar to the one above. Sun Tzu must think this point is very important to reiterate it in chapter five and in chapter eleven as well. This is one of the biggest disagreements between the East and the West. In the West, the company wants to know how many people you have managed in the past. In the ancient China, the commanders wanted to know how well you understand the art of managing even though you have no actual experience.

Asians believe that when someone possesses a high dosage of intuitive knowledge in a particular discipline, it is because she was a specialist in that particular field in her previous incarnations. For this reason Sun Tzu, though a farmer who had never run any army, was employed by the king to be in charge of Wu's army.

To Sun Tzu, managing a million solders was about understanding how one individual works. It is based on understanding human nature. When a million people get together, the group does not take on one million personalities, rather, it takes on one personality. If you know how to handle one person, then undoubtedly, you can manage a million people as a single unit. Sun Tzu's skill of understanding the motivations of people was equal to, and may surpass, any modern psychologist. After all, strategy is primarily about managing people.

My friend Lila is a personal friend of China's Premier Jiang Zemin. Once, during dinner, they were discussing light-heartedly about how to manage China. Jiang Zemin asked her, "How would you do it?"

Lila replied, "I would treat the billion Chinese as if they were my children. By following this principle, China will be well." She is very right, although she never studied Sun Tzu. To her, it was just common sense.

Most persons feel qualified to be a parent, still, it is not that easy to be a good parent. The knowledge of how to be a good parent will place you far ahead of the ordinary managers that learn their management skills from the classroom. A brilliantly creative individual will learn to interleave, by twists and turns, the *fa* of managing her staff with the knowledge of managing her children.

The family unit plays
a critical role in our society
and in the training
of the generation to come.
                    —Sandra Day O'Connor,
                        Supreme Court Justice

EMBRACE YOUR FAMILY AND CAREER

Law and order must be carried out.
The division of your troops' duties, work,
and chain of command must be clear.
Job duties are to be assigned
according to the soldiers' expertise.
—Sun Tzu (1.8)

The working mother's biggest challenge is the balancing of housework, raising children and still delivering an excellent performance at work. A friend of mine who devoted over thirty years of her life to the practice of naturopathic medicine told me, "The biggest cause of women's illness is their children and their husband." It is amazing that no matter how much women work, most of their stressful experiences come from interactions within their family.

It is time for you, the working women, who are creative, innovative and adaptive in managing your offices, to start transferring your skills at work into managing your homes. It is possible to have it all so that you can embrace your husband, kids, and your career—altogether.

Here are some simple steps you may want to consider incorporating into your life.

To manage your family:

• Eradicate the Parasite Syndrome from Your Family Members

Nobody ever said the mother has to do it all. All members of the family are created equal, except for the very young and very old. Train your husband and children to think of themselves as self-sufficient units. They are responsible for themselves. Stop being a slave to your family. Here is an opportunity to demonstrate the power of your leadership.

If, in your household, no one respects you, go back and re-read the chapter titled "Becoming Powerful in Six Short Steps." If you can't get any respect in your own home, how do you expect to be respected, and to lead at work? I have actually known some parents were afraid of their kids. Ridiculous, but true.

• Delegate, Delegate, Delegate

For the common family duties, make a quick list of all the regular housework in your home such as cooking, washing dishes, washing clothes, ironing clothes, cleaning the house, yardwork and so on. As in managing the office, delegate tasks to different individuals. In your home, if you are the better cook, then do the cooking, your husband or children can do the dishes.

If your husband is good at doing the laundry, the kids can fold the clothes, while you iron or take the suits to the cleaners. Together, you can change the beds. Go shopping with your husband or kids because you can enjoy spending that time together.

Once you train your family members to be responsible for certain tasks, the "doing" part is not so hard. What is hard is the time and energy spent in fighting the resistance from those who do not perform their assigned duties. The most important thing in your household is to train everyone to get that they are self-reliant units, and you are not their slave.

It is not optional that they contribute to the well-being of the household. It is their duty to living in that house. They may be able to rotate jobs, but ducking duties is not a viable option. Also, if you explain the necessity of the duties properly, most children will be happy to contribute. It depends on the light in which the situation is presented.

• Let Your Husband See That Taking Care of an Infant Is Good for His Soul

If you and your husband must both work and you also have an infant baby then share the responsibility for taking care of your baby. I once met a couple with a ten month old in the First Class section aboard an international flight. It turned out that the wife was a successful executive and the husband stayed home taking care of the baby.

On this trip he was tagging along, taking care of the baby, so she would not have to be apart from her child for an extended period of time. He said, "Caring for a small infant is really good for my soul as well as for my kid's soul." I heard Carly S. Fiorina, the president and CEO of Hewlett-Packard, tell how her husband is a very happy house-husband.

If you and your husband are too busy to care for a small infant, the best thing to do is not get pregnant until you can afford help to take care of your child. Don't neglect your youngsters, such that they grow up to be added to the countless numbers of tortured souls wandering in this world.

• Keep Your Time Commitment with Your Family

It has been said ten thousand times before and still people don't follow this advice: no matter how busy you are, block out the time you have promised to spend with your kids and/or your husband. If you don't insist on keeping your appointments with your kids, they will become insignificant as soon as something at work comes up. And I promise you, there will always be something "important" coming up at work.

When you start switching your appointments with your kids or lover by scheduling and rescheduling, then apologizing, making promises and more promises, then following up with other broken agreements; before you know it, a simple kids' baseball game will whip itself into a force with a negative life of its own that gets totally out of control.

I knew a lady in the real estate business and, when an offer to purchase a property was calling, she had to go. All of her work resulted in an offer to purchase a property, and in the real estate contract it is stipulated that time is of the essence—she had to present an offer immediately.

In order to not have her children feel disappointed in the event that she could not attend their birthday, she taught them that everyday was their birthday, everyday was Thanksgiving, and that everyday was very special. She would give special parties just for her kids to celebrate being alive. So on the rare occasion where she could not make that "special" event, her children understood that everyday was to be considered special.

• Stay Organized at Home

When your home is disorganized and you can't find anything and bills are piling up at the kitchen table among all the grocery coupons and newspapers from last week, the disorganization itself will evolve into a monster the size of Godzilla.

If you have no idea how to organize your home, pick up some books on the topic of home organization. Harriet Schechter's *Making Time for Love* is a good guide for organizing the working women at home.

• Pay for Your Housework

The majority of the stress in managing a home is caused by your kids and husband not cooperating with their share of the housework. This is followed by screaming at the kids and yelling at the husband. The sink is full of dirty dishes, and the dining table is so full of papers that there is no visible counter top. The house hasn't been vacuumed for four months. Such an environment is a incubator for a stressful working woman and housewife.

The quality of your home life will directly effect the quality of your job performance. An out of control household produces a stressed-out housewife, and thus, an overwhelmed working woman.

If you just can't get your family to help out and you also think you can't afford a housekeeper or a gardener, then you actually cannot afford not to have them. By paying others to do the household jobs, you are actually buying more time for yourself as well as buying a healthy dosage of harmony and peace for your family. You are buying more time to devote to your kids and husband.

She who has whole-hearted support
from all members of her group will win.
　　　　　　　　—Sun Tzu (3.19)

A great Hindu philosopher once said, "He/she who obeys, can command." You will see that by being willing to force yourself to provide discipline and rules for your children and your husband, they will be a happier group, and you will be a happier woman. Furthermore, disciplined people are always happier people. Love your children, but don't be a victim of their manipulation. This is what *fa* is all about.

People think at the end of the day that a man is the only answer [to fulfillment]. Actually, a job is better for me.
—Princess Diana

GETTING PROMOTED

There are six types of terrain:
the friendly terrain,
the steep road,
the complex terrain,
the narrow passage,
the hilltop,
the distant land.
—Sun Tzu (10.1)

In an Ideal world, everyone would get promoted based solely on their performance. And everyone in a workplace would support one another so that each might shine in her respective area of excellence. But as long as human beings are the way we are, the reality of office politics is here to stay. If you are truly brilliant, hard-working and yet you are not getting promoted as you have well deserved, you may want to consider polishing up your in-office political skills.

For most, office politics can cause more pain and stress than their job duties. The anxiety can haunt you at work, and then come home with you to nag you throughout the night. It can even successfully ruin a wonderful weekend with your family. Poor office politics skill not only causes you emotional anxiety, it also hinders your career growth. If you don't know the rules of the game, no matter how brilliant you are, you may get stuck in an inferior post for much longer than you deserve.

I am not talking about making skillful office politics your major objective at work. But, by simply being aware of some of the basic landscapes in your office power struggle, you will come to feel more in control, less frustrated, and more agile at unsticking yourself from the traps that lie along your career path; making you more likely to get promoted into ever higher spheres.

Sun Tzu never spoke on this specific subject, but since we are here to stretch ourselves in becoming wildly innovative, rapidly adaptive, brilliantly creative fun-loving winners, why don't we have some fun stretching Sun Tzu's strategy? Sun Tzu uses these principles to classify terrains so as to effectively maneuver troops through the different geographical restrictions. They can also be adapted to categorize the types of office relationships which exist in all workplaces that we encounter while climbing the corporate ladder.

The formulas listed below are meant not to be taken literally; they are a guide intended to stimulate your perception and expand your vision.

Six ways to maneuver your office terrain:

1. The Friendly Terrain

The friendly terrain is where I can come and go freely. I can set my camp in an advantageous position which assures I will have easy access to defense and offense. Such a terrain is also easy to transport supplies and troops through, which will benefit the outcome of the battle.

—Sun Tzu (10.2)

Friendly terrain is an environment that you can move in and out of with ease. In the office, this means friendly alliances, mentors, a great team; you have the potential for promotion without obstacles; you can move into the position you desire. Friendly terrain will further your career objectives without unnecessary barriers.

Friendly alliances are those who are accessible to you at any time, providing guidance and resolution in challenging situations. You can benefit a great deal by cultivating and associating with such persons, and there are no precautions to take, provided you are a good judge of character. Always analyze people's motives carefully.

The Qualities of an Ally:

• *He or she truly enjoys altruistically helping people with no thought towards reward.*

• *He or she has a special bond with you.* For no obvious reason, this person takes you in. All of my life I have benefited from the generous helping-hands of this type of person. I am indebted to these people who have chanced to cross my path.

• *The expectation of* quid-pro-quo. He or she sees you as someone who is going to be in a position where you might grant future favors or that something you possess is of value to her. This is often not said directly; you will have to use your acute woman's intuition.

Beware of deception. There are treacherous people who will pretend to be your ally, yet, for some real or imagined reasons, she or he will see you as a threat. These type of people pretend to support you so they can keep a close eye on you. They gain access to your work and your mind in order to sabotage you and bring about your downfall.

The simple rule of detecting deceit is: when your gut feeling is telling you not to trust your "supposed" ally while your mind criticizes you for being so hard on others (telling you that you should be kinder and more trusting with people), always trust your gut feeling; not your mind's chattering and reasoning.

2. The Steep Road

> *The steep road is an inclining road;*
> *easy to enter on the down hill,*
> *difficult to exit on the uphill.*
> *If the enemy is not prepared,*
> *you can gain victory through surprise attack.*
> *If the enemy is prepared to do battle with you,*
> *you will be trapped and cannot retreat.*
> *It is often a disadvantageous terrain.*
> *—Sun Tzu (10.3)*

Some job positions are like steep roads. They are easy to get into; it's all downhill. But when you want to move up, your journey is all uphill. This type of position is identified by the fact that you are allowed to keep it as long as no one suspects your ambition.

You must let your boss believe that you are not a threat to his or her position. If he smells just a bit of your ambition and decides to fight you, you will lose. These types of people are in positions of authority above you and they did not get there purely by being nice.

Getting the Best from the Steep Road:

• *If the person that invited you onto the steep road is a luminary in your profession from whom you can learn everything there is to learn about your work, grab your opportunity to learn from the best.* Once you have become one of the best in your business, there is no chance that you will get stuck anywhere.

223

• *After you have learned everything, you may choose to continue your association because, just by associating with your profession's guru, you will gain the imprimatur and bask in her/his glow of reflected glory.* There is also always the chance that your boss-teacher-mentor will want to promote you to head another department or establish a new branch or position in which you can shine. After all, you are her/his prize student.

• *By learning from the best, you will make yourself invaluable to your profession.* You would be considered an asset to any other company, and they would fight to get you. You may then choose to break away from your teacher just as psychoanalyst Carl Jung did. After he had learned everything he could from the great Sigmund Freud, he departed from Vienna to have the freedom to develop his own theories of modern psychiatry.

3. Complex Terrain

This terrain is disadvantageous
for my army to move in and
it is also disadvantageous
for my enemy's army to move in.
In this terrain, even if my enemy
baits me to make a move,
I must stay put.
                    —*Sun Tzu (10.4)*

This type of terrain is full of obstacles such as mental swamps and political division; it is difficult for anyone to function in this terrain. Whoever moves first will lose. Do not let the enemy entice you into action.

In this case, the terrain could translate into an environment where the leader's narrow-mindedness or the impossibility of the project creates an atmosphere of almost certain defeat. Whoever ends up being the aggressive party will be the first to get her head chopped off.

A Survival Guide:

• *The problem with this terrain is so great that the solution does not lie in individual effort.* For those who would rather stay in this un-nourishing environment instead of going somewhere else, all you can hope for is to survive by not rocking the boat too much. The more you do, the more trouble you will get yourself into.

• *Conversely, doing nothing will also not work.* You need to seem to be busy participating, but do nothing that you can be held accountable for. If you survive long enough, the situation may change for the better—maybe the environment will be transformed. The worst that can happen is that you will buy enough time to look for a better opportunity elsewhere.

4. The Narrow Passage

The narrow passage;
when I can occupy it first,
I will guard the opening to the passage
and wait for my enemy.
If my enemy holds the passage first
and is securely guarding the opening,
I will retreat.
If my enemy carelessly
does not guard the opening,
then I shall enter to take the passage.
—Sun Tzu (10.5)

The narrow passage is like the Rock of Gibraltar that guards access to the Mediterranean Sea through the narrow strait between Spain and Morocco. In ancient times, once an army of pillagers had occupied this position, the wealth of the nations that ring the Mediterranean was exposed for their plundering. You must occupy the narrow passage first and then guard the opening to prevent others from entering.

In an office situation there are certain positions close to the key leader; positions (the narrow passage) that strategically contain the power potentially to open doors to infinite opportunities for you. Occupying that post will allow the leader to see you shine. If you hold one of these positions, make sure you guard your post well so that no one can replace you until you are ready to move on to better things.

Strategies for Negotiating the Key Post:

• *If the narrow passage is already occupied, do not recklessly charge in.* You will be killed at the well-guarded passage opening. Do not create direct confrontation with the person who is guarding the passage. By being in that strategic post, she or he possesses the power to harm you—and they will, if they feel threatened by you.

• *The only way you can advance in this terrain is if that person who holds this position does not understand the importance of his post and does not defend the post by exhibiting superior job performance.* He then leaves himself exposed for replacement and defeat, giving you access to the narrow passage.

5. The Hilltop

> *When I am occupying the hilltop,*
> *I must find an easily defendable spot*
> *that provides me with a clear view*
> *of my enemy's activity.*
> *If my enemy occupies the hilltop,*
> *I must retreat or entice them away.*
> —*Sun Tzu (10.6)*

Be the first to occupy the hilltop. Find ground that will provide you with a clear view of all the activities below. The path to the hilltop is normally full of thorny bushes and difficult passages, but, once you arrive there, you became a member of a small, exclusive club.

Consider America's corporate boards of directors, they keep recycling the positions of president and CEO, picking each other to serve as their associate board members. They guard these positions closely so that "outsiders" cannot get in easily. If the hilltop has been occupied, do not conduct a frontal assault and do not fight on their terms.

For those of you who are on the hilltop, your key objective is to secure your control of the hilltop. The best method is to become a skillful warrior and place yourself in a position invulnerable to defeat. The best strategy for doing that is to be excellent in and of yourself, and to show everyone what you are really made of. After all, it took an extraordinary effort to get to the top, now it is the time to show yourself off.

If you arrived here through trickery and truly have no substance, then you are in real trouble. There are many pairs of hungry eyes staring at you, waiting for you to slip.

How to move from second position to first. Everybody has a different personality; there is no one way to get to the top. Take the one that feels more suitable and comfortable to your personality.

The Following Strategies Are for Both Reserved and Assertive Individuals:

• *If you are non-aggressive and you are sitting next to the hilltop, you should make serving your boss and your company two hundred percent of your objective.* The more you do, the more you will learn. Never be afraid to work hard. By so doing, you will be ready when and if your boss is promoted or leaves her job for another post.

You will then be ready and able to take over that position. Although there is no guarantee that you will get the job, you will have doubled your odds by becoming the most capable, suitable person for that post.

• *If your personality is assertive, besides adopting the above method, you should also add a little extra to increase your odds of being the most obvious candidate for moving upward.* Working hard is great, but people do not always notice and acknowledge capable, hard workers.

There are times when you need to give fate a little helping hand. Package yourself with all the whistles and bells, thereby presenting yourself with that glowing halo which entices the power elite to notice you. Besides showing you can handle the job, you also need to look the part.

The top echelon must be brought to think it is better for you to be on their team than to chance losing you to their competitors. They will then extend the invitation for you to reside amongst them on that hilltop.

• *Be sure to not show any signs of threat to the presently occupying forces or you will risk being eliminated quickly.* Wait. Always be genuinely supportive of the one above you whom you serve (and wish to have his job). Also, do not fail to support those people below you who serve you. Having them spread your praises is your best advertising campaign.

6. The Distant Land

*It is hard to fight a war
in the distant land.
It is to your detriment
to engage in such a battle.*
                    —*Sun Tzu (10.7)*

Napoleon, by waging war against Russia, failed. Hitler waged war against Russia and failed. Russia waged war against Japan on the battlefield of Manchuria, China. The superior Russian army was unable to sustain the long supply lines and was defeated by the inferior Japanese forces. Alexander the Great's attempt to conquer India lead to his total destruction. No one successfully wages war in the distant land without a tremendous expenditure of effort.

In the office, figuratively speaking, the distant land is the person who is many levels above you. Stay away from provoking any disharmony with them.

How Can I Eventually Get to the Distant Land?

• *Adopt the strategy of negotiating for the key position in the narrow-passage.*

• *Avoid the complex terrain at all costs if you expect to rise to great heights in your profession.* If you find yourself in this position, find a new job elsewhere, then quit your present job or manage to get yourself transferred to another department.

• *Master making the best out of your steep road situation.*

• *Pray for an abundance of friends in the supportive terrain.*

ↄↄ

> *A good commander must study well*
> *these six types of terrain*
> *and be able to use the principles*
> *freely according to each challenge.*
> *—Sun Tzu (10.8)*

Since you are the Supreme Allied Commander of your life and your career, it is up to you to study well these six types of terrain. When you are facing obstacles you need to first identify what kind of terrain you are in and how you can propel yourself forward.

This chapter is not intended to teach you how to start conflicts, just as Kung-fu is not about learning how to start street fights. The highest strategy is to engender peace and harmony among your office co-workers because where there is harmony, there is prosperity. But when conflicts of interest become unavoidable, it helps to know how to defend yourself and win against adversity. This is the creative adaptation of *fa.*

Chin-Ning Chu

Enemies are so stimulating.
                 —Katharine Hepburn

HANDLING PROFESSIONAL JEALOUSY

*Do not count on the fact that
you are not the object of attack.
You need to strengthen yourself and
prepare yourself mentally
to be the target of attack.*
—Sun Tzu (8.10)

As the great Sufi philosopher Kahill Gibran said, "You work that you may keep pace with the earth and the soul of the earth." Besides financial rewards, the workplace provides us with mental and spiritual satisfaction, and it also gives us the opportunity to keep up with the world. Simply by participating with other people in the workplace, we are keeping pace with the soul of the earth.

A student who attends four years of college, even though she doesn't study superbly, just by attending college, the soul of higher learning touches her. This is the difference between a high school graduate and a college graduate—it is not only about how much you have studied, it is also about participating. Unfortunately, the workplace, besides providing you with the opportunity to keep pace with the earth, also engenders brutal competition.

I really enjoy participating in women's conferences. In these conferences the room is so full of loving and supportive energies. What puzzles me is why women are so supportive towards one another when we are in an artificial, non-threatening environment such as women's conference or when racing a yacht for the World Cup, but tend to undermine each other in the workplace.

I have witnessed this over and over again, from Australia to Europe, in the United States and across the Pacific, crossing cultural and geographic boundaries; women worldwide behave exactly the same. We undermine each other in the workplace. No wonder we do not have an abundance of women in high places.

In one of my women's workshops, when I asked the thousand-plus women executives attendees, "Who is the enemy?" the answer "myself" was put forth with overwhelming agreement, followed by "other women" and lastly "men."

It has been a common experience among women that we are vicious towards one another in the business environment. We may (on the surface) appear nice to one another, but somehow we feel it is necessary to undermine each other as a part of the unwritten rule of competition. We are naturally conditioned by instinct and society to think that other women are a threat to us and, therefore, we are always ready to take down our female competitors.

The Crabs In The Pot

Women practice "The Crab in the Pot" syndrome to keep each other down. When you cook crabs, you don't have to place the lid on the boiling pot—the crabs will not be able to get out. As any crab gets near the top and attempts to climb over the edge, the other crabs will naturally grab the would-be escapee and pull them back to their collective doom.

It is human nature to feel jealous or envy of those who do better at the game of life than us. Everyone has this experience. Only saints and idiots have been spared this torment. But the fires of jealousy burn away our mental peace.

I remember shortly after having arrived in the United States, my (ex)mother-in-law once commented about how much she enjoyed the loveliness of a young lady who had been my exhusband Gary's classmate. Because she showed way too much enthusiasm for this girl, I was offended by how much she went *ga-ga* over this unknown person. I felt competitive towards her.

Many decades have passed and somewhere along the way, I dropped my insanely competitive and jealous nature, little by little. Now, when I see someone who is successful, I see this as a manifestation of the perfect will of the Universe, and I surrender to that divine intelligence which chooses to shower it's glory on that individual.

And I know, according to the divine timing, I will have my turn. In the meantime, I can use another's extraordinary achievement as my inspiration to push myself to do the best I can. I am certain, whether my accomplishment is great or meager, at the moment of my death, my Maker will rate me with equal marks as those great ones who came before me.

I have graciously accepted the challenge of my destiny and, to my greatest ability, I will do the best I know how to make a life for myself while serving humanity towards the highest good. Now, I am happy when I hear of the other "crabs" who are doing better than me. "Go ahead. Go for it," I cheer inside.

Around 1910, the French female screen writer, Francis Marion, came to the film capital of the world—New York City—to seek new horizons. Mary Pickford immediately recognized her talent and insisted on having Francis direct her next film. Mary Pickford sent the studio the ultimatum that if they didn't let Francis Marion direct her film, she would not star in it.

Because of the support of Mary Pickford, Francis Marion went on to became a female pioneer film maker. In a lifetime dedicated to the film business, she helped many starlets became superstars, among those, the legendary Greta Garbo. A great number of women have always been, and will continue to be, a tremendous help to one another.

If you are troubled by some nasty, crab-like creatures, try the following strategies:

• Give the Illusion That You Are Outside of the Pot

Just as crabs can only pull on other crabs who are within the same pot, people can direct jealousy towards you only if you allow them to become close to you. The closer a person is to you, the more likely she will be able to harbor destructive thoughts about you. With socially distant strangers such as Winona Ryder or Elizabeth Dole, we may envy their success, but we rarely experience competitive hostility towards them.

So be sure to keep a respectable mental and physical distance from the aggressive crabs around you. Do not expose yourself to their viciousness by becoming "buddy, buddy" or overly friendly with your office co-workers. The friendlier you are, the more you look like a crab in the same pot. By being pleasant while yet maintaining a distance mentally creates a sense of mystery and illusion—you are outside of the pot; you may not even be of the crab species.

• Slap Her Twice the First Time She Steps out of Line

While the Good Book says turn the other cheek, it also teaches us about an eye for an eye. Both statements are correct. If a child slaps you once, you don't mind it a bit, you may even choose to turn the other cheek just for the fun of it. However, if your office co-worker viciously attacks you, sometimes the most appropriate thing to do is to stop that kind of misbehavior right in the beginning. Instead of turning your cheek, slap her back twice and you will never have to deal with a situation that could, in time, grow out of all proportion if you allowed it to exist and persist.

• Do the Dance Steps of Three Forward and Two Back

If all of the strategies above are unsuited to you, you can always see your encounters with these crabs as a spiritual experience wherein you are learning humility, tolerance, suffering, and endurance. As you are crawling three inches towards the top of the pot while the aggressive crabs are pulling you down two inches, you are still one inch ahead. With persistence, you may crawl your way out of the pot eventually, anyway.

• Support a Co-worker

Even though I have advised you to stay away from aggressive crabs, do not dismiss women allies all together. Support that brilliant, talented lady who is working under you now. Yes, that one, the one that you feel threatened by. Let me analyze this situation from a self-preservation point of view.

Even if you don't support her, with her inherent ability, she is going to thrive anyway. She may well get promoted over you by your boss. Because her talent shines like the sun's rays, everyone else sees it except you who refuse to recognize it.

That makes you look like a small-minded, jealous, threatened fool in your boss's eyes. Worse yet, that talented individual may feel frustrated due to your suppression and take a new job with your competitors. From that position, she can come back to take away your business.

Janet was the editor-in-chief of a women's periodical. Jillian worked as a senior editor at the same publication. Janet did everything trying to block Jillian from being recognized for her talent. Eventually, she made her life so miserable that Jillian reluctantly took a new job as editor-in-chief with a newly established women's publication.

I visited Jillian at her new job. Her new company was well financed. Her enthusiasm was contagious at her office. The morale was high. Consequently, the circulation went way up. Five years later, Janet's publication was sold to Jillian's company and during the cutback, Janet ended up unemployed. Now Janet is working in a lesser position for a non-profit organization.

Take a chance and support another woman. Who knows, by doing the right thing, by adopting the *tao* of support, you may just be saving your own skin.

≈

One who is proficient in the warfare (of jealousy),
is like a snake in the Ch'ang mountain,
she can handle the attack
according to the direction of the blow.
When you strike the head,
the snake attacks with its tail.
When you strike its tail,
the snake attacks with its head.
When you strike it in the middle,
the snake attacks with both ends.
                              —Sun Tzu (11.34)

On your way up, there will always be crabs waiting to oppose you. No matter how vicious they are, as long as you hold to your inner vision and see yourself as the wildly innovative, rapidly adaptive, brilliantly creative, fun-loving winner that you are, no one and no circumstance can defeat you.

As a group, we women had better wise up. It is to our interest, to help other capable crabs get out of the pot first so that they can turn around and help us all escape the steaming pot. This is in line with *tao* and *fa*.

HANDLING PROFESSIONAL JEALOUSY

As a woman, I have no country.
As a woman, my country is the whole world.
—Virginia Woolf

6 WAYS TO AVOID DEFEAT

*There are six ways you can
lead your army to doom.
None of these six ways have to do with
temporal or geographic conditions.
All of these six elements will result
in leading your army to death
purely due to the ignorance
of you, the commander.
—Sun Tzu (10.9)*

In managing, it is as important to know how to avoid defeat as it is to know how to master victory. No one enjoys entertaining the possibility of defeat and yet, without understanding the following six key ways you can be defeated, an ambush is certainly there waiting for you.

6 ways to defeat:

1. Ignorance of Your Resources

> *When the enemy's force is ten times greater, but the commander feels her courage is sufficient to compensate for the immense numeric disadvantage, this commander is throwing her troops into the might of the enemy as if she were throwing eggs against a stone.*
> *—Sun Tzu (10.10)*

When you do not have a clear understanding of your resource limitations and are taking on a project beyond your capacity, you will fail. The reasons you might take on a project for which you are not capable are that:

a. You are eager to show off your ability to perform.
b. You are impatient to be promoted.
c. You are clueless about yourself and your job.

2. Incompetent Management Leading Capable Workers

When the soldiers are superior and the officers are weak,
commands and orders are disregarded.
—Sun Tzu (10.11)

Every working woman has had her experience of dealing with inferior managers. It is most frustrating and demeaning when you, the capable worker, must answer to an incompetent manager. This makes your work unbearably painful.

You can't focus your energy on doing the job, rather, you have to devote all of your mental resources to defending or combating your dumb boss. Your manager's lack of competency will bring down the department. But by the same token, when you are that dumb manager, you can bring defeat to yourself as well as your department.

3. Inferior Staff

When the officers are superior and the soldiers are
inferior, during the battle, the officers will be forced to
throw themselves into the most dangerous duty and will
certainly be killed. Thus, this will lead to the destruction
of all the troops. When a commander is leading
inferiorly trained soldiers to face a superiorly trained
enemy, her soldiers will see the enemy and, following
the blowing of the northern wind, will flee.
—Sun Tzu (10.12)

If the manager is capable but the workers are too inferior to produce the desired result, this will lead to the failure of the project as well as the death of the manager due to overwork.

Once I spoke on a very elite cruise ship, Royal Viking Queen, who catered to the highest of social and financial status travelers. It cost a minimum of US$30,000 per couple for a two-week cruise.

I was with the ship as their speaker for one month, and within this one month, I saw the crew's performance was constantly superior, under very demanding circumstances. I asked the hotel director, "How do you train them to be so polite under such difficulties?" The answer was, "We pay well, and we hire the best people who possess the innate, pleasant personal qualities to do the job."

A natural inclination to do the job well is the first step in recruiting, the next is a proficient training program. If you don't invest in training and the job is beyond your staff's capability to perform, they will feel overwhelmed while facing challenging tasks (strong enemies), and they will quit or look for other jobs.

4. A Manager Inept at Creating Harmony and Unity in Her Department

When the commander is unreasonable
it leads to resentment among her troops.
During the battle, each soldier will
conduct their own war,
instead of obeying the commands.
This will surely lead to defeat.
—Sun Tzu (10.13)

In order for a project to thrive and the department to succeed, support and harmony between the manager and the people are essential. Women within the same office have a greater tendency to stir up trouble by gossiping and passing on negative judgements of each other more than men. If you have a lot of women in your department, beware.

If your manager is a mental alcoholic and tirelessly finds fault with her people or she creates clusters of favored and unfavored groups, then the department's staff will not be able to focus on their job duties. Instead, they will have to play along with the boss's mental games—a sure way to defeat.

5. A Manager Without Power to Discipline Her People

When the commander is weak
and lacks authority over her troops,
when there is no clearly assigned
duties for her staff,
when there is no structure or
organization within the camp,
chaos and disorder will dominate
and defeat will be certain.
—Sun Tzu (10.14)

Although your job title provides the imprimatur of authority and power, the title by itself will not manage the task and the people. The person who possesses the title must execute her given authority to gain the respect.

Lack of power to discipline your people is often rooted in a lack of power within. If you are clueless about your direction, objective, and the ways to get there; if you are suffering from a total lack of clarity within and without; if you are confused about the priorities of your projects and providing foggy direction for your department, you will fail because the chaos will be so great that no one will be able to survive in that environment.

6. A Manager Deficient in Basic Professional Skills

A commander that fails to obtain the proper information
regarding her enemy's strength,
she will utilize a small force to engage a massive enemy,
and order her inferior troops to go against
a superior force.
Due to her lack of attention in training her troops,
there will be no capable soldiers.
                                   —Sun Tzu (10.15)

Carl Von Clausewitz, in *On War,* said, "A commander need not understand anything about the making of a carriage, or the harness of a battery horse, but she must know how to calculate exactly the march of a column, under different circumstances, according to the time it requires."

A manager does not have to know how to do the detail work within her office, but she must know the requisite information about her competitors, understand her limitations, and know how to utilize her resources to obtain the maximum advantage. If you are lacking in the over-all basic skills to perform your job, and yet you act as if it is business as usual—directing this and ordering that, disaster awaits. Everything you do and everything you don't do will both be wrong. If this is the case, then for sure, you are leading your office and yourself to certain defeat.

These are ways to a sure defeat.
It is the commander's responsibility
to make certain that these do not happen.
One must study this with great care.
                    —Sun Tzu (10.16)

All of the above six ways to defeat are human factors, they are all due to a lack of basic professional and human skills. Sun Tzu's management techniques are based on *fa*—the concept of superior training and discipline combined with caring for and respecting your people. Although Sun Tzu's work was written two thousand years ago, we can instantly recognize ourselves and other managers in these situations.

*If you are never scared or embarrassed or hurt,
it means you never take any chances.*
                                    —Julia Sorel

WINNING WITHOUT CONFRONTATION—NEW FEMINISM'S BATTLE

*The strategy that won your victory
cannot be repeated in the same manner.
It should be diversified according to
the specifics of the circumstances.*
—Sun Tzu (6.32)

Those who have fought for the feminist cause are to be commended. All of the women have benefited from their dedication and we are collectively indebted to these brave souls. However, as we entered the new millennium, the old tactics have become outdated and ineffective.

For instance, frontal assault is an inferior strategy now. The easiest war to fight is an undeclared war. We become formless while our opponents are identifiable. We become concealed while our opponents are discovered. We became invisible, while our competitors are exposed. There are the reasons why the old tactics in feminism's battle are out dated and non-effective in the new era.

Waging war against men is an inferior strategy because:

• Winners Do Not Protest

Only the inferior and defeated need to openly protest. In order to win, a woman must win in her mind first, even though she sees no evidence of winning. She needs to keep the mental picture of winning in mind at all times. You must not for a moment be willing to entertain the thought that you are part of a loser's group. Join the winners, don't protest.

• Holding Animosity Towards Men Is Poor Positioning

When you openly declare (by word or deed) that you are bitter toward men for what they have done to women, it only shows you as a resentful woman. Before you even have a chance to fight your battle in the world, you have created unnecessary obstacles for yourself. Men-haters do not make for desirable company in polite society. Men-haters do not make commendable executives in the corporate hierarchies.

• Beating the War Drums Hurts You

In order to maintain a cause, one must continuously look for reasons to sustain her upset and keep her energy of anger alive. It is not good for one's health to harbor so much animosity. In order to sustain the momentum of the cause, one must constantly remember her enemy, contemplating and recreating the rage of being a victim.

This further reinforces the experience of the victim syndrome. What you think, so you become: an angry victim. Being in a constant state of agitation, one becomes easy prey for your competitors.

Instead of beating the war drums, you would be greatly better off utilizing the subtle maneuvering of peaceful strategies to achieve your primary objective—to get ahead; and ahead; and ahead...

• Fighting Affirms Your Own Ill Providence

Words have power: what you say, you become. It can also be very detrimental to constantly remind others that you are the victim of men's discrimination. You become your own bad press agent, frequently communicating that you are a victim.

You are repeatedly reinforcing your inferior position, so, by association, you will become the lady who has been discriminated against. On the battlefield, regardless of how badly you may be losing, never cry out, "Oh dear, I'm losing. My enemy isn't fighting fair."

Inequality is a fact of life—it is up to you to come up with the strategy that will win you the war. When it comes to winning; winning is winning, reasons and excuses are just reasons and excuses. When there is an absence of victory, one clings to reasons and excuses. When you are winning, there is no need for reasons or excuses.

• You Do the Fighting, Others Reap the Reward

The nonstrategic warrior is the one who gets all the battle scars while the others get decorated. You can be a Joan of Arc who crusades for women's equality in your office. You can fight gallantly to remove the conditions of gender discrimination; in the end, the office will not promote you.

Other women will be promoted: the non-troublemakers; the ones who focused on their work; the ones who operated their lives from the position of equality; the ones who saw no discrimination; the ones who exhibited only positive, up energy; the ones who used strategies to quickly move forward—the ones who beat them at their own game.

In 1969, when I had just arrived in the U.S., I didn't know how to drive. I had to get a job close enough that I could walk to work, so I took a position of clerk at a fashion warehouse in Las Vegas. I didn't like how the macho male owner treated the other girls. While the other girls were scrubbing the toilets, I was doing the complaining on their behalf. Within two weeks, I was fired. The owner practiced the strategy called "Kill the Rooster in Order to Frighten the Monkey."

Of course, it was a blessing that I didn't stay on that job and become a fashion warehouse manager. You, however, might have a job that you don't want to throw away so carelessly. If you want to help other women in your office, secure your power position first before helping other mistreated co-workers. Be a strong swimmer first before you attempt to save others.

It is commendable that there are people who are willing to devote their lives to fighting for the woman's cause, wearing the battle scars, since somebody has to do the tough jobs. However, the cream only floats to the top. The people who have benefited the most from the feminist movement are the few professional celebrity movement leaders.

While the foot soldiers have fought the battles, the generals have been getting the medals. I do not want to appear cynical, but you only have so much time and energy in a day; you have to be very practical, asking, "What do I get out of this? Do I get my share of the cream?"

The Non-confrontational Strategies In Our New Feminist Battle:

• Traveling Light

Be so subtle, so small,
you became invisible.
Be so mysterious, so obscure,
you became inaudible.

—Sun Tzu (6.9)

The basic principle of traveling light is so that you may move faster with less effort. If you desire to move up speedily in the world, you need to move as a tight little unit, without carrying extra baggage. Since you cannot take all women to the top with you, you should learn to enjoy traveling light. If you attain a position of power today, tomorrow you will be in a much better position to help your sisters up after you. What at first may appear selfish, can, in the final analysis, be the most altruistic.

It is easier to move an individual ahead instead of a group of millions. Furthermore, if each woman moved herself forward without declaring war by blowing the trumpet of battle, before anyone noticed, peacefully and quickly, a mass of women would be on the top of the professional pyramid.

Try this next time you are walking down a crowded New York City street. If you were to push and shove your way through in an attempt to move yourself to the front of the crowd, you would encounter great resistance, maybe even a punch in the face; expending a lot of effort for meager results.

The second technique is to calmly walk along with alert, watchful eyes looking for openings, and then swiftly move forward to fill the empty spots. Repeat this process as many times as you need to until you have arrived at your destination. You will see how fast you can move forward and leave the crowd behind.

• Operate from a Higher Starting Point

If one is skilled in the strategies of warfare,
she will have the power to impose her will on others,
and protect from others imposing their will upon her.
—Sun Tzu (6.2)

Change the mantra, from "I am an object of discrimination," (even if it is true). Replace it with, "I am equal to all and superior in my uniqueness." Just by declaring internally that you are equal and uniquely superior, you will, in fact, move up instantly without having to do anything.

Instead of insisting you have to fight and scratch your way up to equality, declare your equality. Then, you are there already. You will psychologically find yourself instantly at a higher starting point.

ॐ

Those women who do not consider themselves victims utilize the strategies of guerrilla warfare. They focus on their own strategies for victory; without drawing negative attention, they move up and forward silently. They don't participate overtly in the feminist movement

They see that, from their state of reality, the only road to victory is to treat being a women as an asset instead of a liability. Indeed, being a woman is a great privilege. This is the state of mind of a happy, fun-loving winner.

If we are to achieve a richer culture,
rich in contrasting values,
we must recognize the whole gamut
 of human potentialities,
and so weave a less arbitrary social fabric,
one in which each diverse gift
will find a fitting place.
                    —Margaret Mead

WHERE HEAVEN AND EARTH MEET

*When exercising a military disposition,
it is most important to conceal your intention,
motives and movements from your enemy;
so even the wisest spy
will not be able to see through them.*
—Sun Tzu (6.2)

The principles of *tao, tien, di, jiang, fa* prevail throughout every aspect of our lives. Besides applying to our business and personal life, it applies equally well to everything we do—including the making of music.

The Five Essential Elements In Making Music

Tao Represents the Composer's Creative Expression

Tao is that divine inspiration, that God-given spark of creativity with which you reach for your life's perfect solution and draw to you the magic of universal synchronicity, but only if you are aligned with your own innate goodness.

Tien Is the Musical Timing

Whether a given piece of music will be a hit very much depends on the musical timing. In 19th century Vienna, people's ears were ready for the new sound of the waltz, so Johann Strauss was a hit. In the 1960s, the world was ready for a new sound, so Beatles's music was number one.

Di Is the Available Instruments and Talent for Performing a New Musical Piece

If you write music that requires a certain orchestration and you don't have the instrumentation to produce that sound, it won't work. When Mozart wrote the *Queen of the Night* aria in the *Magic Flute* opera, if he had not been able to find a soprano that could hit those high *g*'s and *f*'s, Mozart would have had to change his composition.

Jiang Is the Conductor, the Leader

The conductor is the one who translates the musical notes into an emotional message, and then directs the orchestra to perform the piece according to his interpretation.

Fa Is the Execution of the Composer's Written Notes and Rhythms That Result from Following the Conductor's Interpretation

Each musician is a self-managing unit. She needs to be good at her musical skill through disciplined practice. Then she must diligently honor the composer's musical strategy and the director's musical expression.

If you are deficient in any one of these five elements, you won't have a successful musical performance. However, the mystery of the five elements are much more than what meets the eye.

The Goodness Of Infinity Meets Finite Human Effectiveness

A few years ago, an Asian reader of mine gave me a piece of crystal framed in a round gold circle with a Star of David in the center. I thought it was strange that she would buy a Star of David. I thought maybe she didn't know that the Star of David was the symbol of the Jewish religion.

Somehow this simple piece of crystal exuded much harmony and love to me; I would wear it from time to time to feel the love from my readers. Now, for the last couple months, I have felt very much attracted to this piece—I wear it continuously, even to bed and bath.

261

During a recent visit to my friends' house, Susan and Greg Bolt of Portland, Oregon, Susan looked at this unique little piece of jewelry and said, "This necklace is perfect for you; this is exactly what you should be."

"What do you mean? This is the Star of David," I said.

"Yes, look at how the top triangle faces down and the bottom triangle faces up. This means that heaven reaches down to earth, and that earth reaches up to heaven. This is the marriage of heaven and earth, the spiritual and the material."

As I am writing this right now, I realize the appropriateness of this piece for this time. Goodness happens out of spontaneity, it is connected to the infinite. Efficiency happens out of planning, it is connected to the finite. By joining infinity and the finite, we thus connect heaven and earth, Womankind and Godhood.

The principle of *tao* and *tien* belong to the goodness of infinity. They are symbolized by the triangle from heaven reaching down to earth. The principles of *di, jiang,* and *fa* are born out of the finite human effectiveness, and are symbolized by the triangle from earth reaching up to heaven.

The marriage of the effectiveness and goodness provide the ultimate winning formula for women becoming all we want to be. However, without your will and your effort, these five elements will remain dormant in your personal and professional lives.

We must have been great souls to be so rewarded as we stand here to witness this glorious time of change. With it, accompanying the world-wide economic reshuffling, comes a great opportunity for all of us to reposition ourselves.

Chin-Ning Chu

"Chin-Ning" in Chinese means "path to peace." She was born in China. At the age of three, Chin-Ning was forced to leave behind her family's fortune and flee to Taiwan as a refugee. In 1969, again, clutching two suitcases, she left home to come to America, struggling with a new language and culture.

Today, she is a renown speaker (see accompanying client list) and an international best-selling author with readers in over forty countries. She is the President of Asian Marketing Consultants Inc., the Chairperson of Strategic Learning Institute and the Founder of Women WorldWide, a non-profit educational organization.

At the age of ten, her primary life's ambition was to be a saint. In high school, she became a novice at a Catholic convent until her father dragged her home. In college, while still a full-time student, she worked for a time as a television soap opera actress, and then as a marketing representative for one Taiwanese and two European pharmaceutical companies.

Chin-Ning's best selling books include *Do Less, Achieve More; Thick Face, Black Heart* and *The Asian Mind Game.* Her work is praised by major media across five continents from *CNN* and major national/international television shows to *USA Today, Asian Wall Street Journal, BusinessWeek, (London) Financial Times,* the international editions of *People Magazine, Marie Claire, Elle, Vogue* and *Harper's Bazaar.*

Chin-Ning has inspired and guided political and business leaders in Asia, Europe and America for the last twenty years. Her readers and clients include England's past Prime Minster, John Majors, U.S. Senator Jack Kemp, Past U.S. Secretary of

State, James Baker, the Prime Minister of Malaysia, Dr. Mahathir, President of Republic of China Mr. Chen Shui Bin and numerous presidents and CEOs of Fortune 500 corporations.

She presents the warrior philosophy as the premier vehicle for mastering strategic thinking in the corporate world as well as daily life. Chin-Ning weaves the diverse elements of strength, strategy, philosophy, pragmatic enterprise and personal growth into every topic she addresses.

She fuses timeless Eastern wisdom with Western practicality into dynamic tools that produce tangible results for solving life's ever-shifting challenges. Chin-Ning is considered the foremost authority on Sun Tzu's *Art of War* strategy. She was the major commentator for *Sun Tzu's Art of War, Discovery Television—Great Books Series*. Through the study of her works, you will discover how strategic thinking can lead you to becoming a wildly innovative, rapidly adapting, brilliantly creative, fun-loving winner.

Partial Client List:

United States

3M Corporation
Aerospace Corporation
Allied Signal
American Association of University Women
American Hospital Association
American Marketing Association
American Organization of Nurse Execs.
American Society of Association Executives
AmeriChoice Health Services Inc.
Animal Air Transporting Association
ARCO Petroleum
American Society of Association Executives (ASAE)
Asian American Hotel Association
Battlecreek Townhall
Better Homes and Gardens
BMC Industries Inc.
Boeing Corporation
California Portland Cement
Carnegie Council on Ethics and International Affairs
Chiropractic Elite Organization
Cincinnati Chamber of Commerce
Clemson University
Columbia Record
Commonwealth Club of San Francisco
Council of Logistics Management

Partial Client List (cont.):

Delaware Valley Minority Business Council
Deloitte & Touch
Employee Relocation Council
Executive Breakfast Club of Oakhurst
Fedelity National Finance
Ford Motor Company
GMAC Home Services
George Mason University
Greater Raleigh Chamber of Commerce
Harvard Business School Club
HCI Publications
Hughes
IBM Business Partners
IBM
International Council on Systems Engineering
Invention Convention
Iowa State Council
Kaiser Permanente
Kaiser Engineers
Kellogg's
Lear Sigler Avionics
Lear Astronics Corp
Levy Strauss
Lewis-Clark State College
Linkage, Inc.
Lockheed Aircraft
Lockheed Martin
Lucent Technology
Marley Cooling Tower
Meeting Professionals International (MPI)

MENSA
Million Dollar Round Table (MDRT)
Minnesota Minority Supplier's Development Council
Monsanto
Motorola
National Council Real Estate Investment Fiduciaries
National Minority Supplier Development Council
National Network of Commercial Real Estate Women
Oklahoma City University
Oregon Marion & Polk County Export Program
Oregon Health Science University
PCS Health Systems
Procter & Gamble
Professional Convention Manager's Association
Prudential Insurance Co.
Ritz Carlton Hotel Group
Royal Viking Queen
Sacramento Chamber of Commerce
San Francisco State University
San Francisco Mayor's Conference
Simon Fraser University
Society for Human Resources Management
South Western Bell
Special Librarian Association
Special Events Magazine
Society for Human Resource Management
SUCCESS Magazine
The Greater Vancouver Chamber of Commerce
The Church of Today

Partial Client List (cont.):

The Strong Fund
U.S. Navy
U.S. Department of Commerce
U.S. Air Force
U.S. Small Business Administration
University California Berkeley
University of California Women Leadership 2000
University of Missouri
Warner-Lambert
Western Legislative Conference
Westinghouse
Whirlpool Corporation
Willamette University
World Affairs Council

International Clients

Alfred Dunhill, Singapore
Asian Business News/CNBC, Singapore, Hong Kong
Australia/Asian Business Consortium
Acer Corporation, ROC
ANZ Bank
AXA
Bank of Bangkok
China Steel
France Telecom
Gold Star Corporation, Korea

Hyundai Corporation, Korea
INSEAD University of France
Lend Lease, Australia
Microsoft Greater China
Nippon Steel
POSCO, Korea
Shell Oil of Australia
Telstra Corporation, Australia
Toyota Corporation, Japan
BHP, Australia
CEMEX, Mexico
China Business Group, Hong Kong, Beijing
De Lage Landen, The Netherlands
Entrepreneur Incubator, Singapore
Grant Hyatt Hotel, Taipei, ROC
Harvard Management Service, ROC
IBM Taiwan, IBM Asia
Know You Seeds, Taiwan, ROC
La Conference de Montreal, Canada
MBF, Australia
Pacific Asia Travel Association
Peru's Executive Summit
Perwira Bank, Malaysia
Postal Service, Republic of China
PTT Telecom, The Netherlands
Quest Consulting Group, Malaysia

WE WANT TO PUBLISH YOUR STORY

Please tell us how you have applied Chin-Ning's ideas and strategies as she has communicated them through her books (Working Woman's Art of War, Do Less Achieve More, Thick Face Black Heart, The Asian Mind Game) which have resulted in a dramatic realization or transformation in your life and/or business.

The length of the story can be as short or as long as is necessary to communicate your complete experience.

Please submit your story in English and mail to:

AMC Publishing
Attn: Editor
P.O. Box 2986
Antioch, CA 94531

(or)

Fax: (925) 777-1238

e-mail: story@strategic.org

For Further Information: (fax, mail, or enter in website)

To: SLI, PO Box 2986, Antioch, CA 94531, USA

Websites: www.strategic.org | www.Chin-NingChu.com
e-mail: cnc@strategic.org
Telephone: (925) 777-1888 ; Fax: (925) 777-1238

Please enter my name in your database:

Name _____

Address _____

Town _____

State/Provence _____

Postal Code_____Country_____

Telephone Number_____

Fax Number _____

e-mail address_____

☐ I would like to receive Dimsum (a free e-mailing of an article written by Chin-Ning, usually on a monthly basis.)

☐ Please notify me for Seminars and Workshops.

☐ Contact me for Chin-Ning to speak to my company/group event (Special consideration/discount for Women's events.)

Product Order Form

Order Line: 1-(925)-777-1888
(M-F; Pacific Time 9 a.m. - 5 p.m.)
Fax Orders: 1- (925) 777-1238

BOOKS:

Working Woman's Art of War HdCvr $19.95 ☐

The Asian Mind Game - Hard Cover $26.00 ☐
Rawsen Assoc./Div. Simon-Shuster

Do Less, Achieve More - Hard Cov. $18.00 ☐
Regan Books/Div. Harper-Collins

Thick Face Black Heart - Hard Cov. $26.00 ☐
AMC Publishing

Thick Face Black Heart - Soft Cov. $14.99 ☐
Time-Warner Books

BOOKS ON DISK:

Thick Face Black Heart $14.00 ☐
on 3.5"Floppy

SCREEN SAVER:

Thick Face Black Heart Screen Svr $29.00 ☐
& 3-D Book on 3.5" Diskette

AUDIO TAPES:

Learning Chinese the Natural Way $109.00 ☐
Eight (8) Cassette Tape Set

Thick Face Black Heart Chin-Ning $75.00 ☐
Live Six (6) Cassette Tape Set

(Over for Continuation of Order Form)

VIDEO TAPES:

Thick Face Black Heart Video $ 24.00   ☐
Presentation by Chin-Ning

Sub Total ☐

CA residents add 8.25% tax ☐

Shipping ☐

Outside U.S.A. ORDERS - ADD Additional $25.00 Shipping

TOTAL ☐

**All Checks, Money Orders, Credit Cards Drawn on U.S. Banks
for Payment in U. S. Dollars**

(☐ MasterCard ☐ Visa ☐ American Express only CCs)

Credit Card # _____

Expiration Date:____/____/_____ (mm/dd/yy)

Name: _____

Address 1: _____

Address 2: _____

City:_____

State: _____ Postal Code: _____

Country:_____

e-mail:_____

Phone: _____ Fax: _____

U.S. Shipping charges:

$ 1.00 - 29.99	$ 5.00
$ 30.00 - 44.99	$ 6.50
$ 45.00 - 99.99	$ 7.50
$ 100.00 - 149.99	$ 8.50
$ 150.00 and above	$10.00

Mail orders to:

SLI
P. O. Box 2986
Antioch, CA 94531 USA

Order Line:

1-(925)-777-1888 (M-F; Pacific Time 9 a.m. - 5 p.m.)

Fax Orders to: 1- (925) 777-1238

NOTES

NOTES

NOTES